STAND UP AND BE COUNTED

THE CARE SERIES

Stand Up and be Counted

EDITED BY LUKE WHITCOMB & NIGEL WILLIAMS

Series Editor
Revd Dr Nigel M de S Cameron

KINGSWAY PUBLICATIONS
EASTBOURNE

ISBN 0 85476 286 8

Printed in Great Britain for
KINGSWAY PUBLICATIONS LTD
Lottbridge Drove, Eastbourne, E Sussex BN23 6NT by
Clays Ltd, St. Ives plc
Typeset by J&L Composition Ltd, Filey, North Yorkshire

Acknowledgements

Much of the material in this book has been adapted from the original CARE Handbook first published in 1987. Acknowledgement is made to those who were particularly involved in that production: Joanna Bogle, Vivienne Bowman, Lyndon Bowring, Nigel Cameron, Charlie Colchester, Candy Elson, Guy Hordern, Ranald Macaulay, George Oliver, Kathryn Porter, Janice Price, Ian Prior and Michael Totterdell.

Contents

Introduction to the Series

All around us, Christians are waking up to their responsibility to *care* — for one another, and for all their neighbours in God's world. The old 'social gospel' has been discredited. It tried to rewrite the message and mission of the church as a social and political programme. Many evangelical Christians responded by retreating into a pietism which denied, in effect, that the gospel had social and political implications at all. But more and more they are being called back to their historic role as the heirs of Wilberforce and Shaftesbury. With a fresh confidence in its biblical mandate, the evangelical conscience has reawakened from its fearful slumbers.

Around twenty years ago, two historic developments marked the beginnings of this decisive move towards the recovery of our evangelical heritage. One was the establishment by the Evangelical Alliance of TEAR Fund, to channel evangelical care to needy people overseas. The other was the setting up of the nationwide Festival of Light — now known as CARE (Christian Action, Research and Education) — to channel evangelical concern for the nation. CARE expressed Christian concern through both practical caring initiatives and public, political campaigning.

The roots of CARE's understanding of its mission lie in our stewardship of God's world (which stems from our creation) and our obligations of neighbour-love (underlined anew in Jesus Christ). We have no option but to care for others; and there are two ways in which we may do so — by practical caring for those round about us, and by campaigning for the defence and enhancement of the Christian values of the nation.

This *CARE series* spans these twin concerns. Some books address major public questions, which may be highly controversial. Others focus on practical issues of Christian caring. We pray that this series will help many Christians think through our obligation to be 'salt and light' in society, as loving neighbours and responsible stewards.

NIGEL M DE S CAMERON

Foreword

This is the book I've always wanted to write! The 70s and 80s were the decades which saw evangelical Christians regain their concern for social and political action as part of their biblical responsibility. From the National Festival of Light in general, and the work of Raymond Johnston in particular, CARE has grown to help equip Christians to participate in political and social action through caring and campaigning.

This book is the fruit of CARE's work in this area. It is a handbook to help those wanting to act but unsure how to go about it. It is intensely practical and does not assume the reader is an expert!

No book will be totally comprehensive in dealing with either the theory or practice of Christian social action, but this handbook seeks to address issues and forms of action not covered in other publications. It draws heavily on the experience of CARE staff and supporters in campaigning on medical and sexual ethics issues for its examples. But our desire is that it should be of value to all Christians, whatever their particular interest—from world development to unemployment—in giving advice on how we can together respond to the challenge of Jesus to be effective 'salt and light' in our society, arresting decay, bringing a godly flavour, exposing darkness and shining brightly to show our nation his way.

May God grant us the wisdom and courage to take up the challenge and do what we know to be right.

Lyndon Bowring
Executive Chairman
CARE

SECTION 1

THE CASE FOR ACTION

1 Why Act?

This is a book about getting involved. It is not a book for the armchair theologian full of good sentiments, whose eyes are closed to events in the world around. Rather, it is for the Christian who believes that 'faith without deeds is dead' (Jas 2:26); who is concerned about other people and the quality of their lives; who cares about issues such as poverty, family life, the nurture of children and their right to life — in short, for the Christian who is prepared to stand up and be counted.

If we will 'be counted', then we will count for something — our voices and actions will have an effect. Too often Christians feel strongly about some issue — whether in politics, local life, or in the school round the corner — but they do nothing. 'I'm just one person,' they say. 'No one will listen to me. How can I change things?' In fact, even one voice raised in protest or encouragement may affect another person's thinking or action. Several individuals acting together may form a delegation or a pressure group to persuade those in positions of leadership that the matter should be taken seriously. And a large enough group may represent a majority of potential votes — something sure to concentrate the mind of any politician.

But while most Christians accept the duty to serve and help other people, mention of politics worries them. 'The church shouldn't be involved in politics,' 'Politics is a dirty game,' they say. Do we have a responsibility to be involved with the workings of the society in which we live? Should we simply seek to help others when they are the victims of injustice or repression? Or do we have a responsibility to try to order our society better?

To try to answer these questions we need to look at the role of the Christian in society: do we really have anything special to offer? Is it really possible to change things? We need also to turn to the Bible, and to seek out the biblical principles underlying Christian responsibility: if we are willing to 'stand up and be counted', we had better be clear why we are doing so.

2 Changing Society

Society is a living organism, and consequently it is always changing and developing. Christians rejoice that they are part of that life, and thank God for both the joys and the responsibilities that result. A society that was static and unchanging would be dead; it is in the nature of things that the customs, manners, and laws of our society are always altering — sometimes minutely, sometimes in obvious ways. We cannot halt that change, any more than we can 'turn back the clock' and return to the past.

However, over the past forty or fifty years, many changes have taken place in Western societies which alarm and dismay Christians. Increasing material wealth accompanied a decline in interest in spiritual matters; the advent of the 'permissive society' of the sixties eroded the conventions which had governed social life for many years; liberation in language and behaviour meant that vulgar or obscene speech and sexual immorality became the norm on our television sets and in the newspapers.

Indeed, an examination of the mass media provides a rough but useful indicator of the nature of a society. How much can a documentary 'get away with' before it is condemned for intrusive investigation of people's privacy? What images are used by advertisers to attract purchasers for their products? Even the most objective television or radio reporting nevertheless reveals a great deal about the fundamental

17

assumptions of the reporter and his audience, and the content of newspapers and magazines tells us something about the moral climate in which they operate.

A more precise view of public morality may be obtained by looking at the laws which are passed in a society, and here, too, Christians in Britain have found much to cause them concern. Changes in legislation have reflected the changes in society's values, and many run counter to Christian principles.

In 1961 the Obscene Publications Act was tested by the publication of *Lady Chatterley's Lover* (the fact that such a book should have been considered obscene at all shows us how much our attitudes have changed in the last forty years). The failure of that test case opened the way for the publication of explicit descriptions of obscene acts, in a literature which is now generally accepted as commercially advantageous. Subsequent Acts such as the Theatres Act of 1968 and the Criminal Law Act of 1977 extended this licence to the theatre and to the cinema, so that there is now very little control over the display of violence, occult practices and deviant sexual activity.

The 1967 Abortion Act affecting the availability of abortion encouraged its use as a form of contraception, challenging the Christian view of the sanctity of all human life. Before the 1967 Act, few doctors approved of abortion, and public opinion on the whole agreed with them. Now, because abortion is legal, many people assume that it is therefore ethical.

The 1969 Divorce Reform Act made it simpler to obtain a divorce, with the result that more and more families were broken up. The 1967 Sexual Offences Act legalised homo-sexual acts between two consenting adults, but had a much wider impact than the decriminalising of homosexuality. It led to the promotion of homosexuality as an acceptable lifestyle. These further devalued the Christian principles of chastity, marriage and the importance of family life. We must be careful, though, not to see morality exclusively in terms of sexual issues. There are other more subtle ways in which Christian principles are being abandoned to the detriment of society.

Society is changing — and these are changes which the Christian must deplore. But we have said that change is inevitable, so what can the Christian do about it? Are we helpless in the face of developments in society? Is it possible for us to influence the changes going on around us, so that they swing in the direction of justice and faithfulness to God's laws?

The lesson of history

There was a time when the world seemed to be changing almost as rapidly as it is today. Back in the nineteenth century, when the effects of the Industrial Revolution were making themselves felt in the squalor of city slums and the depression in agriculture, and in the increasing wealth of the ruling classes, laws and customs were being changed — by Christians.

Life for most people was grim indeed. Working conditions in factories and mines were horrific and the mortality rate was high; child labour was cheap and expendable; the slave trade flourished; for those without work the workhouse was the only alternative to starvation. Small wonder that most adults escaped into drunkenness with whatever money they could earn; gambling, lewd displays in the theatre and cruel blood sports were the favourite leisure activities for those with more money. The rest of society was characterised by political corruption; a harsh penal code and harsher prison system; education which was the privilege of the rich; and the hypocritical posturing of the clergy who preached in church on Sunday and idled with the gentry for the rest of the week.

It was into this situation that what is now known as the

Evangelical Revival erupted. A return to the word of God brought about a fundamental change in the social conscience of the nation through the action of individuals working together. John Wesley had preached not only the gospel of Christ but also the importance of social righteousness: after him came a string of Christian leaders who were committed to evangelism and also to social action. William Wilberforce led a small group of Christians who campaigned throughout the country and worked in Parliament for the abolition of slavery and the slave trade. They successfully changed not only the law but also public opinion over a period of some thirty years. Others (such as John Howard, Lord Shaftesbury and George Muller) effected equally important changes: the prison system was humanised, conditions in factories and mines were improved, education became available to the poor, and trades unions began. They worked in Parliament to change the law, but also through the press and practical action, organising Sunday schools, writing tracts and newspaper articles, campaigning against duelling, blood sports and immorality. The social conscience of the Christian was successfully grafted on to the legal system of the country, and incidentally on to the fundamental attitudes of society.

The great reversal

However, by the early years of the twentieth century, this tremendous Christian involvement had begun to fade away. There were many reasons: some Christians became pre-occupied with the proclamation of the gospel to the exclusion of all else, in the face of the liberal theology which was becoming popular; others reacted against the 'social gospel' which seemed to embrace a humanist social conscience and evade the personal challenge of the gospel; others were affected by the pessimism after the First World War which decreed that society was so inherently evil that it could not be reformed until the Second Coming of Jesus.

Whatever the cause, working through the social implications of the gospel became unfashionable among Christians, and so gradually the influence of the Christian church on society decreased. The effects we have seen. We may well deplore the current trends in public morality and legal ethics; but is there any possibility that we can emulate our forebears of the nineteenth century and bring about such great changes again?

New developments

Voices were raised against this preoccupation with 'saving the soul' to the exclusion of all other concerns, but for many years they were few. However, by the 1960s there was a new mood in society, especially among the young. They rebelled against the materialism of the capitalist Western world, where the new post-war wealth had encouraged people to strive for more and more consumer goods. Some sought escape through drugs; some looked for enlightenment in Eastern religions; those who found their sense of purpose in Jesus Christ found also that the evangelical wing of the church had recovered its morale. Christianity was no longer a middle-class pursuit for those who were interested in salvation alone, in saving their own souls, and indifferent to the plight of the rest of the world: Christians were looking outward again.

In 1966 an American conference on world mission adopted the 'Wheaton Declaration'. This married two aims of 'preaching the gospel to every creature' and 'evangelical social action'. It urged evangelicals to 'stand openly and firmly for racial equality, human freedom, and all forms of social justice throughout the world.'

Perhaps the most decisive move for modern Christians came at the International Congress on World Evangelization which was held in Lausanne in 1974. It produced the Lausanne Covenant which stated 'evangelism and socio-political involvement are both part of our Christian duty', though it gave no guidelines for relating the two issues. Only in 1982, when the 'Consultation on the Relationship between Evangelism and Social Responsibility' produced a report, was any attempt made to grasp this problem. The report suggested that social activity was both a consequence of and a bridge to evangelism: the two are partners because they are united by the gospel. 'For the gospel is the root, of which both evangelism and social responsibility are the fruit.'

At last evangelicals seemed to have taken up the banner of visionaries like Wesley and Whitefield: there was no need to side either with the 'social conscience' wing or with the 'evangelical' wing — the two could be combined. But what, exactly, was meant by 'social activity'? And what did the Lausanne Covenant imply by its use of the words 'socio-political involvement'?

3   What Is Social Action?

The 1982 consultation produced a report entitled *Evangelism and Social Responsibility: an Evangelical Commitment*. Its final chapter was called 'Guidelines for Action', and it made a distinction between 'social service' and 'social action'. It pointed out that social service includes such activities as relieving human need and suffering, ministering to individuals and families, and other philanthropic actions. Social action, however, seeks to remove the root causes of need and suffering, by activity in the realms of politics and economics and by trying to change the structures of society.

John Stott points out that genuine Christian concern inevitably involves both service and action.

> Some cases of need cannot be relieved at all without political action (the harsh treatment of slaves could be ameliorated, but not slavery itself; it had to be abolished). To go on relieving other needs, though necessary, may condone the situation which causes them. If travellers on the Jerusalem-Jericho road were habitually beaten up, and habitually cared for by Good Samaritans, the need for better laws to eliminate armed robbery might well be overlooked. If road accidents keep occurring at a particular cross-roads, it is not more ambulances that are needed but the installation of traffic-lights to prevent accidents. It is always good to feed the hungry; it is better to eradicate the causes of hunger. So if we truly love our neighbours, and want to serve them, our service may oblige us to take (or solicit) political action on their behalf.[1]

23

The role of religion

As Christians we are followers of Christ, who himself 'went through all the towns and villages, teaching in the synagogues, preaching the good news of the kingdom and healing every disease and sickness' (Mt 9:35). Social service and preaching the gospel clearly go hand in hand as we worship our God in the world and try to do his will. We have seen from John Stott's argument above that socio-political action is merely one step further. Yet we have noted that there is still in some areas of the church a deep hostility towards this kind of involvement.

Many Christians have studied scripture and taken the view that we should not be involved with political action or public life; their view has its roots in the earliest days of Christianity when the holy men withdrew from the world and lived in caves in the wilderness. The monastic movement later brought some of them together in small communities, but they held to their principle of separation from the world, a principle which has guided many groups of devout men and women throughout the history of the church. What were the scriptural ideas which lay behind this?

Firstly, the Bible warns us that there is a deep evil in the world order: 'The whole world is under the control of the evil one' (1 Jn 5:19). Since the time of the Fall humans have been in rebellion against the Creator. As a result, when Christians first come to know the redeeming love of Christ, they see their lives transformed, and experience a glorious feeling of deliverance from the old order. They say, 'Our citizenship is in heaven' (Phil 3:20), and so they feel that social involvement can be taken seriously only by non-Christians who do not appreciate the spiritual dimension of life.

This concept of the heavenly home of Christians is at the root of the whole idea of life as a pilgrimage. As Hebrews says of those who have died in faith, 'they admitted that they were aliens and strangers upon the earth . . . they were longing for a better country — a heavenly one' (Heb 11:13,16). This earth is not our home, and we should not become too firmly entrenched here: we are merely passing through.

One further idea taken from scripture is that of contamination — the idea that one should 'keep oneself from being polluted by the world' (Jas 1:27). The Christian may snatch others from the fire, but must take care not to get burnt himself (Jude 23).

It is only fair to present this case against Christian involvement in social action, because as we have seen it does have roots in scripture and many devout and sincere Christians support it. However, the Bible has many positive things to say about the nature of society and our responsibility for it, and we will consider these. Throughout both the Old and the New Testaments we find exhortations for the godly life to be involved not only with worship, contemplating God, but also with the real, everyday world of other people: 'He has showed you, O man, what is good. And what has the Lord required of you? To act justly and to love mercy and to walk humbly with your God' (Mic 6:8). We shall look at the biblical principles in detail in Chapter 4 of this section.

Christian responsibility

Whatever view we take of Christian responsibility, it is immediately clear to us that we exercise it in more than one situation; the Christian is an individual and a part of a church; he may act as a member of one or more groups within that church, as well as outside the church in secular organisations. There are many activities which are better suited to the operation of a group than to the individual, but this does not release the Christian from the obligation to think, to make up his own mind, and to act as an individual where necessary. Indeed, there is one area in which almost all Christians agree that they have a duty to act: voting.

One of the principles of the democracy in which we live is respect for individuals. That respect is demonstrated by the fact that we regularly ask all adults whom they would like to run the country: a General Election implies that everyone's opinion is valid, and that everyone has a right to be consulted about the nature of our community life. G.K. Chesterton once wrote, 'Universal suffrage is an attempt to get at the opinion of those who would be too modest to offer it' — the right to vote gives everyone a role in the ordering of society.

As such, that right is a treasured privilege in democratic countries. Even those Christians who have profound doubts about their duty to be involved in social action nevertheless generally believe that the right to vote should be exercised out of some sense of Christian responsibility. Yet the act of casting a vote cannot really be isolated from all other kinds of political activity simply because it is anonymous. By the action of voting we are implicated in the communal life of our society.

The ballot box is one of the means by which the opportunity for political power is distributed among all citizens in a democracy; it is not an opportunity which we should refuse. The fact that we are offered the opportunity means that we have a responsibility to use it as wisely as we can, bearing in mind our Christian duties of stewardship and neighbour-liness. That responsibility obliges us to be involved, and our involvement cannot stop abruptly once we have exercised our voting rights.

Some Christians avoid political involvement because of the dangers of 'contamination', or from fear of a kind of 'guilt by association' with processes which are not run on spiritual principles. If that were true, it would apply equally to the action of voting, and indeed to almost anything we do outside our church doors. We cannot be separate from the world: but we can try to improve it by our presence in it. Neither can we say that social service is compatible with our Christian beliefs, but that social action is not — for as we have seen above, social action is often merely service taken one stage further, and attempting to remove the causes of hardship, distress or danger.

Indeed, if we do nothing — if we do not even vote — we are not avoiding the issue. The structure of our democracy, giving us the right to choose, means that whether we act or not, we are participating in the process of decision-making. Our passive acquiescence in the actions of others is equally an action, whatever our opinions.

> First they came for the Jews and I did not speak out — because I was not a Jew.
> Then they came for the Communists and I did not speak out — because I was not a Communist.
> Then they came for the Trades Unionists and I did not speak out — because I was not a Trades Unionist.
> Then they came for me — and there was no one left to speak out for me.
>
> (Pastor Niemoller, victim of the Nazis.)

In fact, involvement in political action does not make us 'guilty by association' with wrong decisions, but rather the opposite. We may argue the case for the Christian point of view, and we may then lose or we may win. But whatever the result, our conscience is clear: we have done the best we could. It was Pilate who tried to wash his hands of an unsavoury decision, but history has found him guilty.

4   The Biblical Principles

Before we begin to examine the activities open to us as Christians, in social service or social action, we need to be sure of our basics. What does the Bible teach us about our responsibilities to our fellow men? What are the biblical principles underlying our involvement in the secular world? John Stott has outlined these in his book, *Issues Facing Christians Today*, and we can do no better than to precis his argument here. He takes five great doctrines of the Bible, and claims that we need to understand them more fully, because each of them convinces us of our Christian responsibility.

God

Our tendency is always to limit God to our own interests; we confine him to the observation of our own religious rituals (forgetting how acidly the prophets and Jesus commented on religion which was divorced from real life); we limit him to the covenant he has made with believers (forgetting that he is still the God of creation, who is concerned with the fate of all the nations); we concentrate on the God of justification, having mercy on all sinners (forgetting that he is also the God of justice).

God's concerns are all-embracing: he desires justice not only among his own people but everywhere, in all communities, all nations. If we seek his will, we must be ready to serve it.

Man

Man was created by God not just as a soul, nor just as a body, nor just as a social being, but as all three. So in order truly to love our neighbours, we must be concerned for their total welfare. This is why Christian missions have traditionally included programmes for evangelism, relief and development. No one aspect alone does justice to the nature of humanity.

Christ

To recover a fuller vision of Christ we need to appreciate the paradox of his kingship: the incarnation has practical implications. The Son of God left the glory and power of heaven and entered into our world, to share our weakness, vulnerability, and pain. He served by healing, feeding, befriending, and forgiving, and ultimately by bearing our sins and facing death for us. If Christian mission is to be modelled on Christ's mission, it must mean entering other people's worlds, understanding their needs, and serving them.

Salvation

It is easy to simplify salvation: it may be seen as a self-reformation, forgiveness of sins, or a passport to heaven. Yet it has a wider significance. Firstly, it means the coming of the kingdom of God — God's dynamic rule breaking into our world. The church is supposed to be a model of what a community can be like when it comes under God's rule. Secondly, it means that Jesus is Lord, as well as saviour — Lord of our lives and of our whole experience. Thirdly, it means both faith and love. We are back to the dichotomy of

James — 'faith by itself, if it is not accompanied by action, is dead' (Jas 2:17). The faith which enables us to enter into salvation expresses itself in love, and love issues in service.

The church

Many people mistakenly think of the church as a kind of club, where the common interest of all the members is God. Rather, the church has a double identity — it is at once a holy people, called to belong to God, and also a worldly people, returned to the world to witness and serve. It is a hard balance to preserve: sometimes the church withdraws too much from the world; sometimes it assimilates the world's standards. Yet unless it holds to both parts of its nature, the church cannot affect the world.

John Stott suggests that if we hold these doctrines fully, we must see that the Christian is enjoined to take part in mission, in both evangelistic and social responsibility.

There is a fundamental obligation on the people of God, that they should 'do good' to their fellows. Both the Old and the New Testament require that believers should love their neighbours as themselves, and the parable of the Good Samaritan emphasises that this neighbourliness is to be inclusive — even of enemies. 'Love which is exclusive and limited in its scope is but honour among thieves.'[2] We are responsible for one another.

There are, of course, many other biblical injunctions to action — not least that of Ezekiel: 'If the watchman sees the sword coming and does not blow the trumpet to warn the people . . . I will hold the watchman accountable' (Ezek 33:6). We have a duty to proclaim the will of God, and that includes the principles of social justice. We are to guide our fellow citizens away from danger — physical, moral and social — and towards stability, happiness and security. This is just as much our responsibility as our duty to preach the gospel of personal salvation.

In the New Testament the image of the watchman is replaced by the homely images of salt and light: 'You are the salt of the earth . . . You are the light of the world' (Mt 5:13,14). The salt is a preservative when rubbed into food, and also gives flavour; so the Christian can preserve the goodness and righteousness which exist in the community, and also bring a wholesome and enjoyable flavour to its life. Similarly, Christians must let their light shine so that their neighbours may see their good works and thank God for them. This emphasises the fact that we are not to hide in a corner with our faith, keeping away from the business of the world lest it contaminate us, but to let our activities witness to the love and concern of our Father in heaven.

The Christian is not 'of the world' (Jn 17:16), but Jesus does not allow us to contract out of our responsibilities; he insists that we do his will here on earth: 'My prayer is not that you take them out of this world, but that you protect them from the evil one' (Jn 17:15). We are meant to be in the world, and we are meant to do all in our power to advance the will of God for all people.

5 Priorities and Motives

If Christians are to be involved in politics and social action, we need to establish what our priorities will be. They will not be new to us: Christian principles remain constant in whatever walk of life we find ourselves.

Our first priority is that of worship: love of God comes before love of neighbour. Nothing should obstruct the worshipping community from its first duty of worshipping God — Creator before creature. William Wilberforce was an excellent example of this: in all his work in Parliament and his tireless campaigning for the abolition of the slave trade and the emancipation of slaves, he insisted on his daily times of prayer and worship. This emphasis sets social action firmly in a church context and a proper Christian framework. We should always be asking, 'Where is our love of God in all this activity?'

The next priority is the 'household of faith'. We are to 'do good to all people, especially to those who belong to the family of believers' (Gal 6:10). In other words, if there is a conflict of interests in the individual's life of active goodness (especially where time and resources are limited), the needs of those in the fellowship come first. In terms of local responsibility and the smallest fellowship, the same principle applies: the family comes first. 'If anyone does not provide for his relatives, and especially for his immediate family, he has denied the faith and is worse than an unbeliever' (1 Tim

5:8). We are not allowed to put political responsibility before our family.

After our worship of God and our duty to our family, as Christians we have to remember that we are members of the church, and the first task of the church is to preach the gospel. The New Testament suggests that the greater part of every Christian's time and money should be given to evangelism and building up the people of God.

However, the church may set aside individuals to do particular things. Local councils are responsible for services such as education, roads, and social services; any citizen can stand for election to the local council. The church should prayerfully consider its response when members say they are considering standing for election; will they be encouraged and supported? Will they be released from church responsibilities, such as Sunday school teaching, to free more time? Will they be able to come back to the prayer meeting to report their needs and be confident of getting support?

Not every Christian will be called to this sort of activity, because the apostolic priority is evangelism. Yet churches should surely set some individuals aside in this way to take part in the life and the decision-making in the local community. The life of the church will be greatly enriched if through groups within its membership it can be active in both evangelistic activities and social concern.

Christian motives

Clearly, if the Christian enters public life merely for the sake of fame or social standing, he is no better than the Pharisees. 'So when you give to the needy, do not announce it with trumpets, as the hypocrites do in the synagogues and in the streets, to be honoured by men' (Mt 6:2). The Christian should be looking for appreciation only from God; so how do we ensure that our actions merit God's approval?

There are five motives indicated in the New Testament.

Firstly, we should be trying to be like God himself. 'Be imitators of God, therefore, as dearly loved children and live a life of love, just as Christ loved us and gave himself up for us' (Eph 5:1). Our actions will then be governed by our desire to imitate our heavenly Father, in his unselective love. We will be trying to do good to everyone within our reach.

Secondly, we must remember that we are 'sinners saved by grace'. If we are to reach out to others we need to remember that we too can fail. This will prevent us from becoming proud and arrogant — tendencies which are unfortunately often found in the political world.

Thirdly, we should be trying to obey God's express commands. 'If anyone loves me, he will obey my teaching' (Jn 14:23). That means that even when we are being negative about things, it will be clear that we are not wielding power for the sake of it, nor being a killjoy, but simply being obedient to God's instructions.

Fourthly, we should want to demonstrate the reality of grace and faith, particularly as shown in the second chapter of James: 'What good is it, my brothers, if a man claims to have faith but has no deeds?' (Jas 2:14). If our faith does not issue in loving action we give the watching world every right to doubt our testimony.

Our fifth motive should be to use the gifts that God has given us. 'Each one should use whatever gift he has received to serve others, faithfully administering God's grace in its various forms' (1 Pet 4:10). Like Daniel and Joseph — and even Esther — we should acknowledge our gifts in humility and thankfulness, and accept whatever opportunities come our way to exercise them in the will of God.

6 Christianity in Action

These, then, are the biblical principles underlying Christian social involvement. Yet once we are prepared to take action in the life of our community, we will not necessarily find that all action is political. We must approach our activities in a spirit of willing and prayerful humility, and see where the Holy Spirit leads us.

Some may indeed be placed in positions of leadership; others may find themselves giving those people support, whether in prayer or in practical terms. Some may take responsibility for various tasks within a church or an action group — writing letters, monitoring the press or the local newsagents or video shops. Some people may find themselves getting involved in mother and toddler groups, local schools, or youth work. Some may find that their sphere of activity is their own home, offering hospitality to single parents, lonely elderly people, or families with a handicapped member.

No single task is any more important or useful than another — no matter what the priorities of the world — if we are earnestly seeking the will of God. 'The body is a unit, though it is made up of many parts; and though all its parts are many, they form one body' (1 Cor 12:12). As the body of Christ we are the means by which he can work in the world; we can be the channels for his grace, if we are willing to be used.

So how do we go about it? Where do we start? First, we have to be aware of the needs around us. We have to open the doors of our churches and look outside at the secular world; read the newspapers and watch the television; listen to our neighbours and our children; look around us at the shopping centre and the office and the park. We are part of this community—what are its needs?

Next, we have to pray, asking for the guidance of the Holy Spirit to show us what we can do. And then we can seek out other Christians who share our concerns, to pool our ideas and support each other in prayer. We can gain a great deal from the fellowship of believers.

Finally, we can remember to keep our horizons wide. Too often Christians become inward-looking, concentrating only on the issues that arise in their own church fellowship or immediate community. As Christians we do not belong only to one church or to one denomination, but to the whole family of Christ's followers (including those from traditions other than our own). And we also belong in the world: we are members of our local community, citizens of our country, inhabitants of this planet. If an issue concerns us we may find ourselves lobbying our local councillors, petitioning the government, writing to our member of the European Parliament or even adding our support to international movements such as Amnesty International.

Perhaps we are already beginning to feel daunted again. So where should we start? Where are the opportunities for Christians to be involved in society? Are there practical things that we or our churches can do?

Notes

1 John Stott, *Issues Facing Christians Today* (Marshall Pickering, 1984) pp. 11,12.
2 Nigel Cameron, 'The Logic of Christian Political Responsibility', CARE.
3 ibid.

SECTION 2

FINDING OPPORTUNITIES

1 The Local Community

Issues of national importance can have a certain glamour about them, especially when they are being debated by MPs in front of the television cameras. But often there are glaring needs on our own doorsteps, in the local communities where we live, work and worship. It is these needs which we as Christians and as local churches must also consider addressing.

The paragraphs below offer some ideas as starting points for group action in a local community. It is not an exhaustive list of possible activities, rather a stimulus to thought, research, and prayer.

Debt

More and more families and individuals are suffering from serious debt — sometimes on such a scale that they will never be able to pay off their creditors. Homes are lost when mortgage interest payments rise, or when a job is lost and the rent cannot be paid. Yet still the banks and building societies send out mailing shots offering loans, filled with enticing pictures of holidays, cars or other luxuries. Many people have no idea how to budget, how to plan their finances, or how to deal with the demands of their creditors; often they try to escape the effects of many small debts by taking on a huge loan to pay them off. The loan is generally secured on their home if they have a mortgage, and often at extortionate rates of interest. Some areas have such a poor reputation for loan repayment that they are 'redlined' by loan companies, making it impossible for anyone living there to get credit at all.

- Could you offer a debt counselling service to help people in this situation?
- Could your church organise a credit union, offering loans at reasonable rates?
- Could you campaign for more selective advertising on the part of the banks, or put pressure on your local branch to offer more help and advice to those taking out loans?
- Could you lobby your MP for a change in the law so that extortionate rates of interest cannot be charged?

Elderly people

By the year 2000, more than one million people — that is, one in fifty of the population — will be aged eighty-five or over. The need for appropriate housing and care will be enormous. Too often the elderly who live alone are lonely and afraid; they need friendship as well as physical help. Many find it difficult to manage on a pension.

- Could your group campaign for pensioners' rights, or for reasonable increases in pensions as inflation eats away at the real value of what they receive?
- Could you lobby your local council to provide cheap recreational facilities suitable for the elderly, such as special keep-fit classes, tea dances or luncheon clubs?
- Could you put pressure on the local authority to provide sheltered housing?

The environment

The threat of ecological disaster is well documented now-adays: the problems of acid rain, the destruction of the rain forests, pollution of water and air, the disposal of nuclear waste are all global issues which we may well feel unable to solve. Nevertheless groups such as Greenpeace, Friends of the Earth and the Christian Ecology Group continue to campaign effectively; once they were regarded as cranks: now their views are on the world agenda. But we may still feel that we have more chance of immediate success, and of convincing other people of the possibility of effective action, if we operate first at a local level. What is your immediate environment like?

- Could you organise a litter-blitz, or run a campaign to persuade your local council to erect more litter-bins?
- Could you run a publicity campaign to persuade dog-owners to clean up after their dogs? Could you get the council to fence children's play areas?
- Are there recycling facilities available in your area? Campaign to get some, and then persuade people to use them!
- What about conservation — are there green areas under threat? Is there waste ground which could be cleaned up and used as a wildlife haven?
- Investigate pollution — are your local industries behaving responsibly? If not, could you put pressure on them to do so?
- Does your church support aid agencies such as Tear Fund, Traidcraft, Christian Aid and Oxfam? Could you lobby your MP for an increase in government aid to the Third World?

Family life

Family life is under pressure now as never before. Every day 420 children experience their parents' divorce; one third of those children are under five. About a third of the children lose touch with one parent after a divorce. Is there anything that can be done to help people build stable family relationships, and to support the victims of broken or inadequate ones?

- Does your church offer good marriage preparation, and counselling for those in difficulties?
- Could you start or support a local pregnancy counselling service?
- Could you start a support group for single parents, or provide premises where divorced parents could take their children on access visits?
- Could you start an after-school club for 'latch-key' children?
- Does your town have a non-alcoholic pub or a late-night coffee bar for young people?
- Could you run a toddler group for isolated mums and their babies to meet others?

Health and handicap

At a time when the National Health Service itself is under threat, many of the peripheral care services are in danger of being cut. For those with long-term illness further distress may be caused by these cuts; for those with a physical or mental handicap life may become even more difficult than usual. How much do you know about your community, the care it offers and the problems which occur most frequently?

- AIDS is likely to be an increasing problem everywhere in the future. Could you campaign for more government help and funding, both for research and for practical aid to sufferers?
- Could you organise a series of meetings with a doctor as speaker, on subjects such as stress, drug abuse or other problems?
- As more and more people are discharged from mental hospitals into the community, could you organise some

support for them? Could you raise awareness and allay fears in the neighbourhoods where their homes are set up?

- Could you lobby the local council for more wheelchair ramps and other improved access to public areas?
- Parliament's decision to permit the abortion of handicapped babies without time limit reinforces the idea that they are worth less than other people. Could you continue to make your views known to your MP, while at the same time trying to change this attitude among the rest of society?

Housing and homelessness

With the decrease in the stock of council housing and the influence of the rent act, there is less and less housing available for rent. What there is may be either enormously expensive or in such poor condition that it is scarcely habitable. People moving into an area to find work may be unable to afford a home until they have a job — and unable to get a job because they have no address. How can this vicious circle be broken?

- Could you lobby your local council to increase its housing provision?
- Could you join a housing action group or a housing association which provides accommodation at a reasonable cost?
- Could you campaign for more sheltered accommodation for the handicapped and the elderly?
- Could you organise help for your local night shelter, or start a 'soup run' for those sleeping rough?
- Could you organise a fund in your church to offer 'meal tickets' which could be exchanged at the local cafe?

Local focus

How much do you know about the needs in your local community? Is there an obvious focus of concern in your area which could serve as a starting point? If you have a local prison you could consider the needs of that community — not just the prisoners but the staff. One local Mothers' Union runs a tea bar and creche for the women visiting prisoners. The same group helps with the 'ministry of welcome' at the local cathedral, and opens up conversations with visitors about the nature of faith as well as the style of building.

- Does your town have an obvious focus — a prison, a centre for tourism — where Christian witness could be useful?
- Is there a hospital needing support in the form of local fund-raising or people to visit lonely patients?
- Is there a particular local need, such as an improved bus service, a recreation ground, a school crossing, a child health clinic which could do with your enthusiasm to persuade the local council to act?

The media

Nowadays radio, television, newspapers and magazines are tremendously powerful. They provide information and entertainment, they offer a view of society, they can sway public opinion and change attitudes. If you have a media monitor who is gathering information, you may become aware of the varying standards of reporting in the press.

- If you become aware of political bias, unfair reporting of your campaign or any other issues, could you contact the editor concerned and make your complaint?
- Could you challenge local newsagents about the kind of magazines they sell? (CARE provides 'Family Shop' stickers to distribute to newsagents who do not stock pornographic magazines.)
- Could you write to TV or radio stations if you feel that their reporting is intrusive (for instance, filming or interviewing relatives of victims of accidents, etc.)?

• Could you monitor local video shops to check on their stock and the age of children using them?

Unemployment

At a time of recession, unemployment is a problem which is likely to go on growing. The effects on families of low income and financial difficulties, combined with the trauma of job loss and the loss of self-esteem which comes with long-term unemployment can be catastrophic.

• Could your church offer a drop-in centre offering refreshments, companionship, recreation? Could it extend this pastoral care to advice on looking for work, help with job applications, typing, letter-writing, interviews, etc?
• Could you check whether local leisure facilities offer reduced rates for the unemployed?
• Could you set up an employment scheme such as a neighbourhood co-operative for odd jobs? Government grants are available for this if you can supply the organisation and information. CAWTU (Church Action with the Unemployed) produces a leaflet called 'Creating New Jobs — a guide to help get you started'.

2 Practical Caring

It is good to work together on the large issues, but there are dangers. It is all too easy for the campaigner to talk and work for justice, and to lose the perspective of love; to work for people's rights and to lose sight of the people. The balance can be restored by service — practical action for individuals which forces us to get to know people and share their concerns. So while we are campaigning for better housing, for instance, it's a good idea to spend a couple of nights helping at the local night shelter: it returns our attention from the abstract to the concrete, from the issue to the human personalities behind the issue.

Supposing you want to be a practical helper rather than a campaigner — where do you start? The answer is in many respects the same as for the campaigning group. You begin by educating yourself about the needs in the nation.

For instance, today there are over 1.5 million children living in one-parent families, and we now have the highest rate of divorce in Western Europe. Over one million mentally handicapped people live in our country. Of the 9.7 million senior citizens in the UK one third live alone, and hundreds of thousands of them do not receive a regular visitor. Violence has greatly increased, and the number of recorded rape offences is still rising. Over 170,000 unborn children are aborted every year, and there is a growing practice of experimentation on human embryos and the use of aborted foetal tissue in transplant operations. No one can be in any doubt that we have major problems in Britain, and we need to call on God's help and guidance to show us how to change our world for the better.

So the next step is to pray. Look at your personal world and ask God to show you what you can do.

- Have you ever thought 'I must telephone . . .' and then forgotten to do it? One woman decided that every time she thought like that she would stop what she was doing and act. So often the timing of those calls was significant to the other person — yet each took her only about ten minutes.
- How about putting pen to paper? If you keep a collection of cards and stamps ready then you're less likely to put it off. We may take birthday cards for granted, but an unexpected word can be a lovely surprise, especially to the lonely. Perhaps you prayed for someone and could send them a note to let them know, or let your children draw a picture and send it.
- When you go shopping, stop and think: would an elderly neighbour or a young mum like their shopping done for them — or perhaps to come with you for the company? Including half an hour for coffee afterwards might make all the difference between 'service' and 'friendship'.
- Is there a family outing — a picnic, a trip to the park, playing football — to which you could invite someone who is alone? Inviting someone to share a family meal (including washing-up afterwards!) rather than to 'be entertained' can make them feel welcomed and 'at home'.
- What about being committed to praying for someone regularly this year? Put their name in a strategic place (such as on a mirror) and 'pray in passing'.

These are simple suggestions for everyday activities which fit in with your life. Now what about going one step further, and reaching out a little more?

Christian hospitality

The ministry of hospitality is so sewn into the Bible's threads that it would be difficult, if not impossible, to prove that Christians should do anything other than open their homes to people in need. It is something that seems almost taken for granted — perhaps because it reflects the Middle Eastern culture where entertainment of both friend and stranger is part of daily life.

Certainly there are numerous references in the Bible to caring for visitors. Abraham provided rest, washing facilities and a meal for his unknown guests (Gen 18:1–8); the prophet Elisha was entertained by a poor woman in the village of Shunem, not only with food but with a purpose-built room for overnight stays (2 Kings 4:1–8). But hospitality is more than just a pleasant custom in the Bible: its roots lie in the heart of God who meets people's needs, who shows supreme compassion and love, especially for those who cannot help themselves. In the gospels Jesus speaks of the permanent hospitality of God: 'In my Father's house there are many rooms . . . I am going there to prepare a place for you' (Jn 14:2).

A constant theme throughout the Bible is God's care for the 'orphan and widow': 'A father to the fatherless, a defender of widows, is God in his holy dwelling. God sets the lonely in families' (Ps 68:5–6a). It is because of God's special care for those who suffer in isolation that God's people are instructed to show similar love. There is no discrimination between care for the friend and care for the enemy: 'If your enemy is hungry, feed him; if he is thirsty, give him something to drink' (Rom 12:20).

Hospitality is part of the Christian lifestyle; however limited our means, if we are lucky enough to have a home we can usually manage an invitation for coffee or tea. We can remember to include those who are new to our fellowship, those who stand on the fringe, or those we meet at work who may be lonely. A loving heart and a willingness to do God's will can help us to spot the people to whom we should reach out.

The CARE Homes Programme

One example of an opportunity for demonstrating Christian hospitality is the CARE Homes Programme, a network of Christians throughout the UK able to provide short-term accommodation for those in need. Some of us may be able to offer more than just fleeting contact to the lonely people we meet. A spare room, space for an extra chair at the table, room in our family life to include an extra person — perhaps we can find ways to share our homes more fully. The young man who has never known a secure family, the depressed mother who has been deserted with her children, the fearful girl who has been banished from her home because she is pregnant — can we reflect God's loving heart and open our homes to them?

The CARE Homes Programme is a network of Christian homes throughout the UK able to provide short-term accommodation to those in need. Each home is placed on the register after a careful assessment procedure. The host family indicates the type of guest they are able to accommodate and the length of stay they can offer, depending on their individual circumstances.

A young pregnant girl requested a placement with a CARE family as the relationship with her mother was not good and was deteriorating. A co-ordinator visited the home and discussed the matter with both the girl and her mother. After an initial weekend visit with the prospective family, the girl stayed in the CARE home for the duration of her pregnancy.

Although all the placements are into Christian homes, CARE is willing to try to help anyone regardless of class, colour or creed. If placed, the guest lives in the home as part of the family and contributes to his or her keep. Placements are not made overnight: arrangements and introductions are made carefully, with time for either party to withdraw if they decide it isn't going to work. It is important for the family to know something about the person they are considering taking into their home, though of course there are some things CARE interviewers are unable to establish — like whether the person ever takes a bath!

Usually the guest visits the family for a weekend initially, and after that clear guidelines are drawn up about the length of the stay and the expectations of both sides. From these tentative beginnings, many happy and long-term relationships have been established. Very occasionally a placement breaks down — either because the guest leaves voluntarily, or because they are asked to do so. It is important to remember that the guest is a guest; if the person is causing serious disruption to the family life of the hosts they must be asked to leave — though in that situation the CARE co-ordinator would be on hand to support and advise the family.

> Living in the inner city in a block of flats, a young Christian couple on a very low income requested a summer holiday for themselves and their two young children. They went to stay with a CARE family in July.

A constant stream of people in need are contacting CARE, anxious to spend time in a Christian home. They include pregnant girls, single parents, widows and widowers, handicapped children and adults, elderly people, unemployed men and women, and others.

As far as the Homes Programme is concerned there is no

> A girl who had been in trouble with the law was placed in a CARE home for three weeks' convalescence after medical treatment. Her host writes: 'How wonderful it has been to share our home with J for three weeks. I am aware that the Lord was preparing the way even before your phone call . . . God has made it a time of blessings all round.' This girl actually became a Christian while in the home and is now being cared for by a church in her area.

limit on the number of people who can become involved. There is no doubt that there are enormous numbers of people in need in our country. The danger is that we become hardened to the needs we see on television or in our newspapers. Perhaps we think that someone else, some-where, is doing something about it.

But the welfare state has always had holes in it, and for a multitude of reasons people fall through. CARE does not assume that someone else is doing the caring; God's work depends on the goodwill of individuals who are prepared to act.

One carer who has opened her home to others gives her point of view:

It's not been easy to find time to write these few paragraphs. Christmas is a busy time, of course, but with five extra bodies in the house at the moment, a few minutes peace and quiet are hard to find.

The extra bodies are a mum and her four children, aged between one and fourteen, who are staying with us to escape from a situation of domestic tension which was becoming unbear-able and was causing the mother serious depression with all its attendant problems. It has been lovely over the past weeks to see these symptoms gradually disappearing.

It's about eighteen months since we were first accepted for

CARE's Homes Programme and this is our third set of visitors. Each time it's been a Christian mum and her family needing to get away from difficult home circumstances. The first arrived with one child, the second with two, and this time it's four! What will it be next time?

So what does it cost to take someone into your home? It costs time. Those chats and cups of coffee when you really had something else you wanted to do. It costs privacy when you just want to sink down in a chair with your husband at the end of a hectic day. It costs prayer and worry as you get involved in a situation over which you have little control. It costs effort as you cook and plan for an extended family, and patience when the children don't behave as you think they should. It costs our own three children too, as they share their home, their time and their parents, but it's taught them a lot and on the whole they've enjoyed the experience.

We've been fortunate to see rewards from our labours. Prayers have been answered, lives have been touched and solutions found. Not that we would claim there are easy answers to the problems, or that our visitors have gone home to lives of bliss. They will all still have battles to fight and difficulties to face, but God did provide for them when the going was getting too tough for them to bear, and we are thankful to have been a part of that provision.

So why did we get involved in the first place? What are the qualifications? Well, we have no qualifications at all except a reasonably sized house, a happy, stable family, and a real appreciation that God has been so generous to us that we have no right to hold on to it all for ourselves. Of course, you need God's guidance to get involved in something like this. We'd had a sneaking feeling for a long time that we were being called to use our home in some way, but the clear guidance came when we were really willing to be obedient.

3 Schools

The upbringing and education of children is a responsibility placed by God first and foremost upon parents. In our complex society we have set up schools and colleges to deal with those areas of education which are generally beyond the scope of the family; and our churches usually make some provision for teaching children about the faith. In practice, the education of our children is a partnership effort involving home, church and school — though it may be worth reminding ourselves both that the ultimate responsibility before God rests with parents, and that most children in our society do not have any church links.

This chapter does not attempt to deal with the legal requirements affecting schools, nor with the kind of schools which are available; some sources of information are suggested in Section 5 Resources. Rather, it looks at some issues in education, and some of the courses of action open to Christians. All schools are required to produce a prospectus which in future will include a statement of the values which underpin the school's spiritual, cultural, moral and social life as well as its academic life. The assumptions and beliefs behind the whole curriculum and ethos of a school have a powerful influence on the attitudes to life and the choices that our young people make, as well as their academic progress.

In examining education issues, and in particular, in looking at schools, Christian parents need to ask themselves the questions 'What do we want from our schools? What are our priorities in education?' Talk about 'standards' often causes confusion, and it helps to distinguish three things which a school can offer:

- academic excellence and achievement;
- firm discipline, good outward appearance and pleasant behaviour;
- spiritual and moral standards firmly rooted in Christian teaching.

All three are no doubt desirable, but they do not come together automatically as a package. The best academic school in your neighbourhood could be a spiritual disaster area. It is essential to sort out your priorities prayerfully before you make choices as a Christian parent. The current government is taking steps which it believes will enhance the choice available.

The dangers of secularism

In a country where only about ten per cent of the population think of themselves as 'regular churchgoers', and considerably fewer claim to be 'committed Christians', it may seem unrealistic to expect a Christian education system. Yet, for reasons of history and tradition, many Christians do expect just that. Our education system owes much to Christian pioneers, and to the local groups of Christians who established thousands of schools in the nineteenth century. Certain patterns of teaching and behaviour established then or earlier (such as the daily Christian assembly) were slow to change, and Christians were perhaps lulled into a false sense of security.

In recent years, however, this pattern has begun to change — partly, perhaps, because of the many schools in some urban areas with a high proportion of children of other religions, but also (and more often) because schools reflect the adult world, where Christian commitment is rare. About a third of all the state maintained primary and secondary schools in this country are 'voluntary' — that is, they were established by voluntary bodies: the vast majority of them (over 7,000) by either the Church of England or the Roman Catholic Church. These schools have direct links with their parent church. However, the remaining county schools, especially at secondary level, have very often moved away from any claim to be Christian. In spite of the 1988 Education Reform Act, which attempted explicitly to restate the place of Christianity in religious education and school worship, there are few signs that Christian attitudes are being taught in schools.

Many of the issues which worry Christian parents may be seen as symptoms of the general process of secularisation. The school day for many pupils very seldom begins with Christian prayer; sex education is given in ways which Christian parents often find unacceptable; occult literature and teaching makes its way into the classroom. These examples are the ones that appear most obviously to Christians, but the teaching of history or science, for example, is likely to be equally, if more subtly, secularised. No aspect of education is value free.

In many schools the old Christian traditions have been replaced by a broadly 'humanist' philosophy. This has several features: first, it stresses the essential 'niceness' or 'reasonableness' of people, which, it is suggested, will naturally lead them to form a considerate society. At the same time (and perhaps inconsistently), the idea of any absolute standard of moral behaviour is rejected. The autonomy of young people, their right and ability to choose for themselves, becomes a central aim, and in this setting, religious belief is seen as a private matter, where different people come to different conclusions, all equally valid. In addition, of course, there is widespread ignorance on the part of pupils and teachers alike about what Christianity teaches.

This mixture of vaguely humanist assumptions and lack of Christian commitment produces a variety of problematic situations.

When teachers without any faith of their own attempt to lead multi-faith approaches to religion, confusion is bound to result. It may be suggested, sometimes quite dogmatically, that all religions lead to the same goal — a claim clearly at variance with most of the religions themselves. Schools may engage in the celebration of festivals of different faiths, which can involve the children of Christian families in acts of worship which they see as worship of false gods.

There may also be difficulties in lessons other than RE. Material concerned with the occult may easily be introduced into the classroom as resources for creative writing or other activities. Horoscopes and literature featuring witches or evil spirits may be used without any warnings about the dangers of evil spiritual forces.

Sex education, too, presents problems, from junior school onwards. It is becoming rare to find a Christian view of sex being seriously advocated outside a church school, and on the whole, the secular values of the world prevail. This means that sex outside marriage is accepted provided that contraceptive precautions are taken, and it may be suggested that homosexual practices are normal.

More generally, humanist assumptions about human nature and morality mean that many moral issues are sidestepped in schools. Where nothing matters except personal freedom, there are no absolute standards of right and wrong.

Practical action

So what can the Christian parent do? First, in relation to the specific difficulties outlined above, it is worth being aware of the parent's right to withdraw a child from RE or assembly. This should always be seen as a last resort, as it is likely to make the child feel conspicuous and lonely. The first step should always be to discuss your concern with the child's teacher and head teacher (and in doing so it is important to remember that a child's account of what happens in lessons may not always be accurate!)

However, if you are seriously concerned, for instance, that your child is being asked to take part in an act of worship in another religion, you may well want to withdraw. In that case, talk first to a trusted leader of your church, and check with other Christian parents, who may not be aware of what is happening. Joint action by a group of Christian parents is more effective than a solitary protest: a group of children will cope better together in this situation; a head teacher will take much more seriously the reaction of half a dozen families; a group of you can take action together in prayer; and if you are from different churches, your action will be seen as having a wider base.

Similarly, if you are concerned about the subject matter of other lessons, you should always ask for an interview with the teacher and put your views courteously. In the matter of sex education, it is the governors of each school who have responsibility to consider its content and organisation. As they produce an annual report and hold an annual meeting of parents to discuss it, it is a simple matter to get this issue aired in public.

Other, less precise concerns — such as the suggestion in science lessons that 'science has disproved the Bible', or about the content of books being read in literature lessons, need careful consideration. (See the Christians in Education papers Science Education and A Great Gulf Fixed on these two topics.) Discuss matters first with the children, if they are old enough to understand your concern, and then with your education group at church. If you eventually decide that the book in question or the presentation of lessons is definitely 'anti-Christian', then you should seek an interview with the head teacher.

Fortunately, however, we are not usually concerned with 'dealing with problems'. The Christian, whether a parent or not, who is concerned about the life and atmosphere of our schools, will be interested in taking practical action to help them. Some ideas are outlined here which may provide starting points for individual or group activities.

Prayer

A prayer group may consist of Christian parents from a variety of churches, whose children attend a particular school, or it may be based at your church and include church members who are interested in education issues. In either case, you need to get to know your situation properly before you can pray intelligently.

A good beginning is to identify the education professionals in your congregation: listen to their concerns and difficulties. Could you offer them a telephone 'hot-line' prayer service (always with due regard for confidentiality) for crises? Treat them as your 'front-line' people and support them in prayer. The 'professionals' in your church, however, in modern Britain, are quite likely to be teaching other people's children in schools some distance away. Making contact with the teachers, Christians and otherwise, who teach the children of your own church and its locality is clearly just as important, and will often require a separate effort.

You need to be familiar with the local schools and their particular areas of need. One supporter of Christians in Education wrote:

> After Spring Harvest 1986 we felt we ought to take a more active interest in our children's schools, especially the secondary school which our daughters attend. Therefore we contacted two teachers who we knew were Christians and several parents who attend local churches. Each month so far we have seen progress on at least one issue for which we have prayed. These include: heading off Halloween as a topic for assembly; the implementation of the new GCSE Religious Education syllabus; prayer for several new girls who were very apprehensive about joining the school;

concern about some of the books used by the English Department which include stories of witchcraft, etc (we haven't tackled this directly yet); that the CU should be recommenced (and it has); guidance on how to get fathers more involved and how to contact other parents.

If you are a parent with children at school then you probably already have a great deal of basic information, and visits to the school and conversations with teachers and others will give you an idea of the school's main needs and opportunities, and its spiritual 'climate'.

Head teachers, including some who are not themselves committed Christians, may welcome the idea of people praying for the school; some teachers have asked for prayer for particular needs or situations. If your praying group finds it difficult to get together because of other responsibilities, you may find it easier to set aside a regular weekly time of day when everyone agrees to drop what they are doing and pray together. Such a group still needs information, and a distribution of a prayer letter may help.

Practical care about schools must be based on serious intercessory prayer, as a foundation for all other activities.

Voluntary help

There are many opportunities for parents to offer voluntary help in schools — these may include practical help (the construction of buildings, apparatus and equipment, from covering books to building a swimming pool); fund raising (to provide equipment and additional facilities); assisting teachers (in the classroom, library, games lessons or on visits); and organising or helping with out-of-school clubs.

Even if you have no specialist skills you can still offer help which will be greatly appreciated. No one is asking you to replace the teacher, who is the professional, but he or she may well be very glad of the offer of another pair of hands to clean the paint pots, cut up paper, hear children read, or put away equipment. If you can give some time on a regular basis you can provide a valuable starting-point for your church's ministry to the local school. You will be showing practical care in a way that will win you respect and trust within the school community.

It is important to note that this kind of help must be given in a genuine spirit of service; it should not be seen as a way of 'getting in' so that you can 'preach the gospel'. Schools are about education, not evangelism, and non-Christian parents do not send their children to school to be evangelised. If schools are willing to accept our help we must take care not to abuse the trust they place in us.

Of course, this does not mean that we have to conceal our Christian faith either from teachers or from children. When you are established in a school and have won the confidence of the staff it may well be that teachers or pupils will ask you questions about Christianity, either from curiosity or from personal need. Even so, you need to be sensitive where children from non-Christian backgrounds are involved.

Regular help in the school may be out of the question for most people, but occasional evening or weekend help is something many more parents can give. Fund raising and other activities in support of the school need reliable workers, too, and a Christian presence here is important.

Joining the PTA

The parent-teacher association varies from school to school: in some places it is primarily a fund-raising organisation, in others it comments on and helps with all aspects of school life. Even if in your school it seems to be the former, your involvement is still valuable. Your willingness to participate in fund-raising and other practical activities gives credibility to your contribution to other issues, and your views are more likely to be taken into consideration. One parent writes:

Active involvement in the PTA has enabled me not only to participate in fund-raising events, but to contribute to discussions about curriculum, communication between school and parents, equipment and resources, etc. When it was suggested that a parent run an after-school club for Dungeons and Dragons, because I was there, I was able to explain why this was not something we should encourage in the children, and followed it up by giving the PTA chairman and the head teacher a copy of the Evangelical Alliance publication, *Danger: Children at Play*. As the school reconsiders its policy on sex education I have been able to suggest this is an item on which parents should be consulted and proposed that it be an item on the agenda for the meeting between the PTA and school governors.

Showing appreciation

One important way of demonstrating our care for schools is by showing our appreciation for the many good things they give our children. Teachers do not always feel valued by the community: Christians, sadly, are among those who often take them and their commitment for granted. When a teacher organises and runs a long day's trip to some place of educational interest a warm word of thanks or a bunch of flowers can do a lot to signal our gratitude and boost morale.

Secondary teachers who give up lunch hours or marking periods to give extra coaching do not normally expect to be rewarded, but they would certainly be heartened by some personal indication of gratitude for their efforts. One church wanted to show its appreciation for the work done by a local middle school, and after some delicate inquiries presented the staff room with new coffee making equipment — an imaginative gesture of thanks.

A knowledge of the school's needs and a tactful approach are always essential if you intend to give any sort of gift. Money is almost always welcomed, and so are gifts of good new books to school and class libraries. (CiE has a list of recommended children's literature)

It is most important to talk over your ideas with the head teacher first.

Churches and schools

Before we can pray intelligently, think clearly or act decisively about any issue, it is important for us to have as wide and deep an understanding as possible. This is certainly true in the field of education, where issues tend to be exceptionally complex, and the information given in the media is frequently over-simplified. If your church decides to start an education monitoring group, it should if possible include some people who are engaged in professional teaching, some parents whose children are still at school, and one or two members of the church leadership who are able to take a detached view. A subscription to a journal such as the *Times Educational Supplement* will provide material for discussion and keep you abreast of developments.

Your group can put education firmly on the agenda by arranging a special occasion in a service — an 'Education Sunday' or something similar. Then you can keep it there by a regular 'education spot' in worship, house groups or prayer bulletins.

An education group can take a long-term friendly interest in local schools, building relationships and being available in a spirit of service. It is most important to remember that all church/school links need careful handling: schools are often sensitive (sometimes with good reason) about church 'interference'. Many head teachers, however, would welcome offers to lead school worship and you may be able to offer your premises, with hospitality, for RE visits, carol services, or other events.

If a school does come into conflict with Christian teaching, you can help parents to co-ordinate their complaints and actions in response.

One area where your work overlaps with that of the schools

is with your young people. Have you ensured that your youth programme, if necessary, offers 'supplementary education' schemes based on Christian thinking? You can give your young people the Christian world view — something which few schools would now attempt.

Voluntary Christian groups

At the same time you can encourage and support school CUs and Bible Clubs with prayer, offers of speakers, and perhaps finance and resources. Too often Christian parents or churches have been glad to know that a CU exists in a school, but have not given any practical support. School Christian groups always need informed prayer, and can often make good use of gifts of videos, help with printing attractive programmes, or even a place to meet out of school hours. To give the right sort of support to a school CU will probably mean contacting its leaders and the staff who help, and getting to know their situation. They will benefit from knowing that local churches support them — could you offer them a five-minute presentation in a church service, to share their needs and hopes with your fellowship?

School worship

The 1988 Education Reform Act restates the duty of schools in England and Wales to provide for daily religious worship to be available for all pupils (subject to a parental conscience clause). It further specifies that this will be of a 'broadly Christian' nature. While this has created some difficulties, it has also opened up many schools to offers of help from the local Christian community. Churches and Christian youth organisations which have established good links with schools are being flooded with requests to lead worship, especially where there are few staff who feel able to lead Christian acts of worship. This kind of help needs to be given with care and sensitivity; schools will not welcome mini church services, nor high-powered evangelism.

School visits

As part of their religious education programmes, schools will often arrange visits to places of worship. The kind of reception they receive will make a great impact on both children and teachers. There are several points to consider.

- Take the initiative by inviting local schools to your church — not only for educational visits but also for special occasions such as carol services or harvest festival.
- Make an educational visit to your church memorable by arranging a properly conducted tour, prepared in advance. Use it to explain your forms of worship, the meanings and use of such items as pulpit, communion table, baptistry or font.
- Arrange beforehand with the teacher organising the visit for a brief (five-minute) talk by someone about what church membership means to them. The church building is the base of a living Christian community, and the children can be helped to understand this.
- Be welcoming; don't expect visitors to know the etiquette of behaviour in church. Aim to make them feel they would like to come again. Drinks and biscuits over a question time in a church hall or room offer a positive way of concluding a visit.
- Ensure that all visits are prayed over by the church.

If we wish to exercise a legitimate Christian influence on our local schools, it is important to build as many bridges of friendship, co-operation, appreciation and helpfulness as possible. The more we go out of our way to be openly supportive and positive about the good things schools do, the more they will be prepared to listen and act when we find it necessary to question school policies which run counter to our Christian commitment to our children.

Becoming a school governor

In 1988 the Education Act provided new opportunities for parents to work more closely with teachers and education authorities. As governors, they now have a much greater say in the running of their children's schools, and have a stronger voice on governing bodies which are no longer dominated by local education authority representatives. Many Christians become school governors by other routes also. Elected teacher representatives may well be Christians, as may the LEA representatives, nominated by political parties. The 'community governors', co-opted by each governing body, very often include representatives of the local Christian community. The governing body produces an annual report, and all parents have the opportunity to discuss this at an annual meeting.

The job of a school governor offers an ideal opportunity to be closely involved with the school attended by the children of your church. Christians have the chance to identify with their local community and to act as 'salt and light' within it. As governors, they come into contact with many parents, as well as teachers and local administrators, and thus they can learn about the needs and concerns of other people, and have the opportunity to influence these situations for good. Governing bodies are now one of the chief agents for holding schools accountable for what they do.

Who is suitable?

The sort of person who is needed to be a governor is one who cares, and who is willing to be an active participant — you should not underestimate the amount of time needed. You should be prepared to take the job seriously, because it is a great responsibility to be called to represent others in such a vital area as the education of children. You also need the ability to communicate, and to be a good listener, to be willing to ask questions about matters you do not under-stand and not to be put off easily! Above all, you need to be ready to take matters to God in prayer, and to listen to the promptings of the Holy Spirit when you ask for guidance.

There is a great deal of help and advice available, both from schools and local authorities, and from Christian organisations. Christians in Education can put you in touch with other Christian governors (from a mailing list of over a thousand), and runs courses on the work of governors, many of them in co-operation with the Association of Christian Teachers.

Procedure

If you wish to become a parent governor, the first step is to contact your child's school to find out when the next election will take place. At the same time, find out exactly what is involved — how long would you remain in office? How many meetings are held, when and where are they held, and how long do they usually last? What other responsibilities would you be expected to take on? You should also discover what method of election is used, and how parents are informed about the elections beforehand.

Once you have definitely decided to stand as a candidate, you may find it helpful to discuss the matter with your minister or church leader — your church will want to know what you are taking on in order to give you full support, especially as you may have less time for church activities.

The next step is to put your name forward formally as a candidate (the school will inform you about the details of local procedure). You will certainly need to be proposed and seconded by other parents, and it may be that a group of Christian parents from one or more churches can collaborate over nomination.

If you wish to explore the possibility of becoming a local authority nominated governor, it is sensible to begin your enquiries through the local organisation of the political party you belong to or support. Teachers in a school elect their own teacher representatives. Suggestions for the co-option of community governors will usually be made by the elected and appointed governors, including those from the school (head teacher and teachers). It is a good starting point to be known by a school as someone who is interested and prepared to give positive support and time to the work.

One word of caution: being a governor assumes a concern for the whole life of the school: positive support for good things and a lively interest in all that is happening are essential. A Christian governor needs to be a real friend to the school. Work as a friend, and your voice will be heard more effectively on those occasions when you have to challenge something.

It is vital that Christians should grasp this opportunity to be involved in the environment in which our children learn. Do consider whether you are called to this important work, and ensure that your church education group and other Christians are aware of forthcoming elections.

The arrangement for the government of schools is different, with school boards rather than governing bodies. CARE can advise further how Christians in Scotland can make the most of the opportunities open to them.

Christians in Education

Much of the information in this section was made available by Christians in Education via George Oliver, former Director of CiE. Christians in Education has now become a department of CARE alongside Caring Initiatives, CARE Campaigns and CARE for the Family. George Oliver writes:

> As we seek, as Christians, to become positively involved in the life and work of our schools, we need to look closely, with informed thought and prayer, into the issues. The 1988 Education Reform Act begins with a strong statement about the need for a properly balanced curriculum to promote the 'spiritual, moral, cultural, mental and physical development of pupils at the school

and of society'. We shall need to ask probing questions about how far and in what ways both national and local educational policies are promoting spiritual and moral development.

In all our educational concern we need to adopt a fully Christian approach. It is all too easy for us to limit our interest to what is happening to our own children and those of our immediate family and Christian circle. We need perhaps to remind ourselves of the implications of such a verse as Philippians 2:4, 'Each of you should look not only to your own interests, but also to the interests of others.' In our society there are all too many without the power or ability to ensure fair treatment for their children. An Old Testament verse may be our necessary reminder of our own responsibilities towards them: 'Speak up for those who cannot speak up for themselves, for the rights of all who are destitute. Speak up and judge fairly; defend the rights of the poor and needy' (Prov 31:8,9).

4   The Political Arena

The world of government can appear intimidating and remote to many citizens. But there are practical ways in which we can seek to influence government decisions. After all, the political system in the United Kingdom has been deliberately designed to give everyone a share in the decision-making process.

Through intercessory prayer, campaigning on specific issues, involvement in political parties and standing for public office, the Christian community can act as a force for good within the life of the nation, and as a restraint against evil when and where appropriate.

This chapter looks at each of these areas from the Christian citizen's point of view and also includes a brief explanation of how decisions are taken at the different levels of government — local, national and European.

Praying for those in authority

When we pray for local, national and world leaders, we are combining two biblical concepts of power: the human in a position of influence, and the ultimate authority of God.

Scripture leaves us in no doubt about Christ's unique position in the universe. Colossians 1:16 tells us that 'things in heaven and earth, visible and invisible, whether thrones or powers or rulers or authorities; all things were created by him and for him.' When God raised Christ from the dead he seated him 'far above all rule and authority, power and dominion, and every title that can be given' (Eph 1:21).

So when we pray, we are turning to one whose supremacy over the human and spirit world is indisputable. Yet we are always aware that our earthly world is ordered in such a way that human leaders are set over us, and so we ask a sovereign God to bring about his will through those leaders. As we submit ourselves to him and discover his will for the nations, we have the privilege of sharing with him through our intercessions.

There are three reasons why we should pray for those in authority, outlined in Paul's instructions to Timothy:

> I urge, then, first of all, that requests, prayers, intercession and thanksgiving be made for everyone — for kings and all those in authority, that we may live peaceful and quiet lives in all godliness and holiness. This is good, and pleases God our Saviour, who wants all men to be saved and to come to a knowledge of the truth (1 Tim 2:1–4).

It is true, of course, that at times of persecution the church often seems to be strengthened; nevertheless, the work of evangelism and building up the church is very much easier in a peaceful and godly society. Civil unrest and war seriously hamper the proclamation of the gospel, and rioting or imposed curfews restrict opportunities for preaching. During wartime it is often impossible for missionaries to reach certain areas. A tranquil lifestyle in a country makes it easier to preach Christ than when people are living under the threat of invasion. In any case, a state of emergency absorbs the resources and the efforts of the authorities so that other important matters are neglected. Prayer 'that we may live peaceful and quiet lives' is also prayer that we may have strong families, healthy community life, and a prosperous and secure nation.

The second reason for praying for our leaders is that we

may live our lives 'in all godliness and holiness'. If a nation is no longer God-fearing, all kinds of priorities, from justice and equality to mercy and welfare, begin to crumble. It becomes difficult to make people aware of Christian truth, and this affects the general direction of the nation's development. The people in authority can undermine or foster respect for God by their philosophies and the stances they take. For instance, if the Shops Bill (allowing Sunday trading) had been successful, it would have implied that commerce was more important than spiritual and recreational life, and further devalued Christian beliefs and standards in people's minds.

We looked briefly in the first section of this book at the changes which have taken place in society over the last forty years, and the results of legislation which has been passed. There is a clear need for prayer for a return to righteousness within the nation, especially among those who are responsible for making our laws.

We need to pray not only for national leaders, but also for those in local government. Some developments in local councils may become sufficiently widespread to have national importance, if we do not see the implications and speak out locally first. For instance, some local councils have drawn up policies which state that practising homosexuals must not be discriminated against in terms of employment, membership of clubs, etc. Any charity or church failing to implement a policy of equal rights for those in a homosexual lifestyle could lose charitable status and even forfeit civic protection. If this charter were to become enshrined in law, the church in this country would enter a period of unparalleled persecution; also, the nation would experience further moral decline as homosexuality becomes seen as normal.

City libraries and information centres have allowed periodicals and magazines promoting other religions and the occult to be displayed, while stopping any publicity of Christian activities: a church has already been refused permission to use council property (including parks) for open-air witness and evangelism. This kind of ban will inevitably spread to other places unless Christians work against such decision-making and pray for those in authority.

In obedience to Paul's injunction to Timothy, our prayer list should include MPs and councillors, managers of the media, industry and commerce, the leaders in unions, civil services, education, health and social services. Police, magistrates and judges equally play their part in affecting the spiritual well-being of our nation. We should also remember our church leaders, and pray that they will give fearless moral and spiritual guidance to the people.

The third reason for our prayer comes at the end of the passage, where Paul adds that God wants all men to be saved and to come to a knowledge of the truth. All Christians should address themselves to the issues of peace, morality and social justice, but we should never forget our commitment to the Great Commission of Matthew 28: 'Go . . . make disciples . . . baptising . . . and teaching' (Mt 28:19,20). Our leaders can help to create the right atmosphere for sharing the good news of the gospel, and we must remember to pray for this, too.

Further practical advice on prayer is given in Section 3.

Campaigning

CARE's Parliamentary Constituency Programme

CARE organises a nationwide network of campaigning groups (known as 'Core Groups') based on Westminster parliamentary constituencies. Core Groups comprise Christians from a variety of local churches and fellowships. Each Core Group seeks to:

• pray for the nation, the local community and those with local political responsibility, eg local councillors, the MP, the MEP;

- learn about some of the contemporary moral issues facing Britain;
- inform local Christians about contemporary moral debates, so that a considered and timely response can be made;
- influence public policy through pressure, persuasion and participation in the political process, with the emphasis placed on action.

The centres of political power with which Core Groups are principally concerned are local government, Westminster, Whitehall and the European Community. Some Core Group members go on to join political parties and stand for public office.

The portfolio of issues includes pornography, family policy, human embryo research, abortion, euthanasia, Sunday trading, education and broadcasting. The common thread is a concern for the sanctity and dignity of human life created in the image of God, and the well-being of children and families. Core Groups are encouraged to be involved in a range of activities concerning these issues, including national and local campaigns using all the techniques outlined in earlier chapters. In particular, great care is taken with the campaigning style: the aim is to lovingly confront secular values and institutions while persuading others to support Christian principles and practice. Harsh attitudes and violent demonstrations are always avoided.

The constituency programme is co-ordinated from CARE's office in Westminster, five minutes' walk from the Houses of Parliament. In Northern Ireland, Scotland and Wales a Regional Director is available to advise on regional issues. Action undertaken at a local level by Core Groups is supplemented by the work of the CARE team in London. CARE is not aligned to any one political party, and the team help sympathetic MPs and Peers from all the three main parties. Party policy is supported only where it clearly supports the main objectives of CARE.

'The Core Group has kept me involved with all that's going on. If I can't personally come to a meeting, the newsletters that are sent out are brilliant because they stimulate me to write . . .'
'I'd never written to the Prime Minister before . . .'
'You get more involved with your MP.'

Core Groups are kept informed about what is happening nationally through regular campaign updates, and CARE staff are on call to answer queries personally. A wide range of materials is available, as well as training in campaigning methods.

Political activities

Many people associate CARE's political work with high profile activities, when legislation is going through Parliament. However, progress is only made through relationships, lobbying and briefings which often involve long-term persuasion of MPs. For instance, on the issue of pornography CARE has initiated:

- a crucial meeting of over fifty MPs and Peers looking at the effect of pornography on our society, particularly as it affects women and children — key speakers included the Head of Scotland Yard's Obscene Publications Squad, a therapist who works with sex offenders and a specialist in child abuse;

- numerous Parliamentary questions and correspondence with government ministers, drawing the attention of Government and Parliament to the obscenity issue;

- an Early Day Motion which called for research into the impact of pornography, signed by over 240 MPs from all parties (one of the largest numbers for an EDM since 1979) — as a result the Government commissioned a major study by the Home Office;

- fringe meetings at the main party conferences;
- private meetings with MPs from different parties;
- lobbying of government bodies like OFTEL about telephone chat lines.

Tackling your MP

One very effective way of making the Christian viewpoint heard is to communicate with your local MP. Practical advice on how to do this is given in Section 3.

Joining a political party

In the first section of this book we looked at the Christian's responsibility to become involved with politics, whether by campaigning in a Christian group or by personally taking part as a decision-maker. It was pointed out that unless Christians are willing to give up their time and energy and join political parties and stand for election, there will be no hope of ever achieving a Christian presence in Parliament or in local government.

When considering which political party to join we should remember that no party will offer an ideal environment in which to practise our Christian faith: we simply have to find one which agrees best with the policies we favour.

We need to examine both the national and the local situation when we are looking at political parties. The best way to follow national policies is to read up the debates that take place in Parliament. These are recorded in part in some national newspapers, and in full in Hansard (available from HMSO or from your local reference library). TV programmes also give exposure to political personalities and policies, especially the live broadcasts from the party conferences each autumn. Many monthly and weekly periodicals contain useful political information.

The national situation, however, is only the sum total of a large number of local situations; sufficient involvement at a local level will eventually change the national shape of a party. Each of us lives in a Ward, and the major political parties are usually represented in each Ward. It is worth while visiting the chairman or secretary of the local party association and discussing issues in the local area; you may find it easier to relate to a party over local concerns such as schools, housing and education.

There are many important opportunities offered when you become a member of a political party. Firstly, membership gives you the right to vote on issues which need to be decided, to join committees formed for specific purposes, and to participate in the formation of policy at all levels. In particular it provides a chance to share in the selection of candidates for election at local and national levels.

Secondly, it gives you the opportunity to exercise your personal influence. Integrity of character and balanced judgement are qualities highly valued in many areas of politics, and a Christian who demonstrates these could well be entrusted with the responsibility of office, which widens the sphere of influence.

Thirdly, it may lead to selection by the local association to contest an election at the local or national level. This offers the possibility of exercising your Christian values in government, as a member either of a controlling group on a council, or of a majority party in the House of Commons. The task is immensely demanding but also richly fulfilling: you have the chance of establishing 'government by God's standards'.

The working of the political parties

The Conservative Party
Graham Webster-Gardiner writes:

> The Conservative Party is short of members, especially active members. Each constituency has a local Conservative Association which has considerable autonomy to run its own affairs. The local

agent, if they employ one, will be delighted to sign up a new member because you will be helping to pay his salary. If he finds that you are also prepared to work, then he will make sure that you soon find yourself on a committee, or two, or more.

The usual structure is for the constituency association to be divided into wards or branches based upon a geographical split, sometimes coinciding with local government boundaries. Joining the local ward committee would be automatic for someone who is interested in politics and indicates a willingness to put in some effort on the doorstep or with the social activities of the branch. Becoming an officer of the local ward is easy as there are usually few applicants. It is the officers of these wards who form the executive committees for each constituency, and it is the executive and constituency officers who form the management committee which runs an association. For a person with any vigour it should not take long to get on the constituency management committee.

Real competition will probably emerge only when one wants to become a constituency officer such as chairman or women's chairman, or chairman of the local Conservative Political Centre — the most political of all the groups in the local Conservative Association. Even then the competition will not necessarily be intense.

There is some power residing at this level, including the key matter of selecting candidates for local government and, once in a while, Parliament. The selection of motions for party conferences can be heavily influenced by a keen and active officer. It is the chairman of an association, however, who will through area meetings and liaison with the local MPs have a real chance to discuss and influence policy. Within the Conservative Party, certainly at area level, there is competition for the various offices, as it is from the area level that the national committees emerge; and these do have a real influence on the party leaders, especially those in Central Office.

If that is where your interest lies, progress in the voluntary side of the party needs to be made at area level and above. The workload of the chairman of an association can be very heavy, and a Christian needs to consider the best use of his or her time when thinking about taking such a post.

Age and gender are no drawback. By the age of eighteen I was constituency vice-chairman of a large Young Conservative branch in Croydon North-West; by the age of twenty-three I was the national senior vice-chairman of the Federation of Conservative Students; and by the following year the chairman of the Conservative Political Centre in Croydon North-West, which also made me a constituency vice-chairman of that association. In subsequent middle age I have, among other things, been the deputy chairman of the Epsom and Ewell Constituency Association, whose chairman was a lady. There are many active women in local Conservative Associations; their activities are not confined to the women's division.

There are, of course, other ways in which one can be involved in the Conservative Party, including joining one of the pressure groups.

The Labour Party

Guy Tolmarsh writes:

There are many ways to get involved in the Labour Party. You need to be tough-minded and sure of both yourself and God's calling: being a Christian and trying to change the system will bring you up against opposition. Whichever party you support, you will probably be criticised by both sides.

The structure of the Labour Party is complicated and can be a barrier to involvement; to penetrate the system patience is essential. All members are part of a ward branch, based on the council wards. Meetings are usually monthly. Wards elect delegates to the Constituency Labour Party (CLP) General Committees (GCs). CLP-GCs also have delegates from other bodies such as unions and co-operative societies, and delegates can be mandated to support policies at a higher level. The Labour Party is based on a delegate committee structure which is broadly democratic. Accountability is an important part of the structure; it is ineffective to be an individualist or a maverick. There are many committees, all with executives and sub-committees, and to get acquainted you will need to attend many boring meetings. Often small groups exert an undue influence on the party, because there are so few active members, especially in cities.

The best way of getting started is just to get involved as a servant. Activities include preparing election and campaign leaflets, canvassing, secretarial work, fund raising, helping with advice surgeries and offering friendship. In this way people get to know and trust you, and you get the opportunity to understand situations and learn about the other people in the party. To start with just be helpful; when you feel confident in relationships you can begin to push for those changes which God has suggested to you. You may be surprised at which people become allies and which enemies — when you start to be more active, things often get tougher.

Policy formation arises through committees by resolution. A ward party can influence policy through the system, but this route is difficult. The only way to influence policy at a national level is through organised campaign groups. Local influence is easier, but you have to be patient and learn the ropes. The pinnacle of party policy formation is the production of manifestos. Local Authority manifestos are put together through Local Government Committees (LGC) or District Labour Parties (DLP). To the outsider this can appear to be a mystical ritual: the aim of anyone seriously trying to influence this must be to watch, listen, get involved and learn the way in, and then act. At a national level things are more complicated: the annual conference is the supreme policy formation body, but for pragmatic reasons it can be overruled by the National Executive Committee (NEC) and the Parliamentary Labour Party (PLP). Block voting and the methods of arriving at decisions are changing; lobbying and letter-writing can influence policy.

Labour Party Councillors are usually nominated from the wards or other branches and then interviewed by the DLP executives before selection (in cities the interviewing is done by LGCs). In some places (which shall remain nameless) you can become a candidate as long as you can breathe. Becoming a parliamentary candidate is more complex. Every egotist in the party aims at this, and at the last count there were over twenty thousand aspiring MPs. If you are a Christian, selection takes not only time and patience but also God's almighty hand.

The Liberal Democratic Party

George Kendall writes:

The Liberal Democrats pride themselves on their democracy: their leader is elected by the entire membership, and members are encouraged to contribute to the policy-making process. A Christian, joining the party because of their existing ideals, also has a chance to help develop these ideals.

Christians can become involved at every stage of the policy-making process. They can join one of the societies devoted to thinking through issues within the party; there are already Christians in the leadership of most of these groups. It is from the discussions of these groups that much of the party's policy comes.

Policy ideas have to be refined and worked through, and members with specialist expertise can apply to join the working groups that develop draft policy papers. After being approved by the Policy Committee these papers are debated at the party conference, first in draft form, and then in a definitive version.

All members have the right to speak at consultation sessions at party conference (another source of policy ideas), but if they become voting representatives of their local parties, they can also speak and vote during the policy debates at conference. This party conference is the sovereign policy-making body of the party.

Christians who are not interested in grand speeches and discussions with the party's leading thinkers may prefer to contribute through the Liberal Democrats Christian Forum. This group is not a lobby; it involves Christians of all denominations with different opinions on many subjects. Through its newsletter, and day conferences and meetings at party conferences, the forum gives its members a chance to discuss politics from a Christian perspective, and, more importantly, to meet like-minded people. These contacts can help members of the forum to put motions to party conference in their own name.

Those thinking about joining need not worry if they disagree with some of the party's policies. Debate is welcomed; there will always be disappointed minorities after every contested vote; but then everyone will some day be disappointed with a conference decision. Joining the party must, of course, involve commitment to the ideals of the party: it would be futile, as well as dishonest, to join simply in order to influence party policy. However, if a new member does have reservations about some of the party's policies, he or she has the right to try to change them.

It isn't easy to influence party policy, but with hard work, persistence, and a desire to persuade rather than dictate, it can be done. Liberal Democrats respect tolerance, and a willingness to see both points of view; they also respect integrity. They particularly respect members who are not just interested in policy, but give time and energy to help the party in its election campaigns.

Becoming a councillor

Councillors have many opportunities for providing leadership in important areas of policy and management of local services. Millions of people are dependent on the performance of councils for the quality of vital aspects of their daily lives.

There are several phases in the process of becoming a councillor; the first may be called the information phase. Your first step is to discover which councils are responsible for the delivery of services in the area in which you live: Regional, County, Metropolitan District, Borough or District.

The next is the nomination phase: in order to comply with the law all candidates must be validly nominated. Nomination papers must be given to the returning officer (who is responsible for the conduct of the election) at least four weeks before the election day. The candidate must have a proposer and a seconder and be supported by eight others. All ten must qualify as voters in the ward where the candidate is seeking election, though the candidate does not have to be a resident in that ward. The candidate must also appoint an agent who will be responsible for the conduct of the campaign, with particular emphasis on the keeping of financial records. Great care should be taken to ensure that you follow the strict rules governing election campaigns.

The political phase requires you to decide whether to stand

as a member of one of the main political parties, or as an Independent. Hundreds of Independent councillors are returned to office time and time again, so it is not vital that you belong to a political party. However, the party machinery and organisation can provide considerable support and encouragement to a candidate, as well as being a source of local knowledge. The party often has a political statement which applies to the whole council, and support and advice will be offered by candidates in neighbouring wards.

The object of the campaign phase is to gain more votes on polling day than any other candidate. The campaign is usually concentrated in the four to six weeks preceding the day of the election, and may include meetings, door-to-door canvassing, leaflet distribution and many other activities. The culmination is the count of votes to decide which candidate is successful.

Once elected, the councillor begins the representation phase. It is necessary to have a thorough knowledge of the ward and to meet the leading personalities as soon as possible. Only if you are knowledgeable will you be able to take the initiative in situations which demand change. You will also get to know many individuals who ask for help on particular matters.

Councils do their work in committees, and each member sits on a number of them. The political party which has a majority effectively controls the council, and this group elects the council leader; it also ensures that it has a majority on all the committees (thus controlling the decisions) and appoints one of its own members as chairman.

There will also be work to do in the local ward association of the political party, and in the group of councillors who are of the same party. In addition, councils often appoint members to outside bodies such as Health Authorities, voluntary organisations, etc. All this has to be done in your 'spare' time, or such time as your employer will allow you for council duties.

There is a growing number of Christians serving as

councillors throughout the country, but the nationwide need is urgent. Many Christians are able to serve their communities in this way, and should pray and consider whether God is challenging them to come forward. If you really don't feel that you are called to this, could you offer support and encouragement to those who are?

The structure of local government

The information given here is merely an outline of local government as it is organised at present, to enable you to understand the various levels and their responsibilities. Local government in the UK is a tiered system, with several layers of government piled on top of each other (the Isle of Man and the Channel Islands operate differently).

Parish or Town Councils

This is the smallest and most local level of government in England and Wales, but it does not exist everywhere. The 10,000 Parish or Town Councils are organised on a county basis, and information can usually be obtained from your local Secretary for Local Councils. A Parish Council consists of a chairman and not less than four councillors; elections are usually held every four years. The council must hold a public parish meeting once a year at which local affairs are discussed, though most of its legal powers have been abolished. Its duties may include the provision of shelters, village halls, street lighting, car parks, playgrounds, and so on. It may also administer local charities and have miscellaneous powers relating to rights of way and planning applications.

In Wales every district consists of one or more areas called 'communities' which have community councils run on similar lines.

District Councils

This is the next tier of local government in predominantly rural areas; in urban areas the equivalent is the Metropolitan District Council. The whole of England and Wales (excepting London) is covered by these authorities. In Metropolitan Districts, councillors are elected for a term of four years and one third of the council retires in three of the four years; in non-Metropolitan Districts, councillors are also elected for four years, but the District Council has the choice of whole-council elections every four years, or election by thirds as for Metropolitan Districts.

District Councils control such affairs as airports, baths and pools, car parks, museums, planning, public transport, cemeteries, electoral registration, markets and fairs, parks, housing, refuse collection, licensing cinemas and sex shops, etc. Metropolitan Districts have similar duties but are also responsible for education and social services.

County Councils

The final tier, which only operates in those areas where there is a District Council (ie not in those urban areas where there is a Metropolitan District Council) is the County Council. In England and Wales there are 47 County Councils.

County Councils consist of a chairman and councillors; each county is divided into electoral divisions, each of which returns one councillor elected for a period of four years. County Councils are responsible for planning, national parks, traffic and transport, highways, caravan sites, education, housing, social services, police, fire service, weights and measures, public libraries, museums and galleries, and refuse disposal.

London

Local government in London is organised differently through the London Boroughs which have responsibilities similar to those of the Metropolitan District Councils.

Scotland

In Scotland the tiers consist of community councils (which are optional and have no statutory functions); 53 District Councils which are responsible for local planning, housing, local health and amenity services and building control; and 9 Regional Councils which deal with strategic planning, transport and roads, industrial development, police, fire, education and social work. Orkney, Shetland and the Western Isles have all-purpose authorities because of their remoteness from the mainland. Councillors are elected for four years.

Northern Ireland

In Northern Ireland there are 26 District Councils and 9 Area Boards; District Council members are elected for four years. There are 4 Area Boards for health and personal social services, and 5 for education and public libraries.

Public services

There are some government services which are locally delivered outside the framework of local government: these include the health service and police. Provision is frequently made for local government representation on the local boards of management responsible for the delivery of these services. This means that local councillors can often make a valuable contribution from their knowledge of local needs.

The Houses of Parliament

The progress of a bill through Parliament

Parliament is made up of the House of Commons and the House of Lords. Its primary job is to make the laws which govern our national life. A law in draft form which comes before both Houses of Parliament is called a bill. Here are all the stages a bill has to pass through in both Houses before it becomes a law or an act.

First reading of a bill   Most bills are introduced in the House of Commons by a Minister of State on behalf of the Government of the day. The 'first reading' is put on the Order Paper (the Parliamentary agenda) for each day. In practice the first reading is a formality and involves no debate. The Clerk just reads the short title. The House then orders the bill to be printed and fixes a day for the second reading. A Private Member's Bill will be introduced by the sponsoring MP.

Second reading of a bill   This is the stage at which the general object or principle of the bill is debated fully by the whole House. At the end of the debate a vote is taken on the bill and if it passes then this is a fairly reliable indication that the bill will become law if it is a Government bill. In 1986 the Shops Bill failed at this stage in the House of Commons. MPs rejected the principle of unrestricted trading on a Sunday. Many Private Members' Bills, however, get a majority at second reading only to fall at later stages usually due to a lack of time to complete all its stages. If the bill is passed it is committed to a 'Standing Committee'.

Committee stage of a bill   The Committee goes through the bill clause by clause, examining each one in great detail. Members of the Committee propose amendments which sometimes are debated for hours and consequently this stage may take many weeks to complete. CARE regularly submits amendments to MPs. The MPs who serve on the Standing Committee are chosen by the Committee of Selection. The Committee of Selection is a group of MPs given special responsibility by the whole House of Commons to decide who serves on the Standing Committee for each bill. They work in close co-operation with the sponsor or Minister responsible for each bill.

The Committee of Selection appoints MPs to serve on a Standing Committee for a particular bill who have special

qualifications and interest in the subject of the bill. The composition of the Standing Committee will reflect the vote on
second reading. This Committee does not meet on the floor
of the House of Commons but in a Committee Room specifi-
cally designed to mirror the House of Commons though in
smaller form. The Committee is presided over by a Chairman
who is an MP and who acts in the place of the Speaker.

When the Standing Committee has completed its consideration of the bill it then goes back to the whole House
of Commons for Report Stage.

Committee Stage in the House of Lords is different to the
Commons in that any Peer who wants to can take part in
Committee Stage. Also Committee Stage takes place on the
floor of the House of Lords.

Report stage of a bill This is when the conclusions of the
Standing Committee are reported back to the whole House
of Commons. Report stage offers further opportunity to
amend the bill and any MP can table (put forward) amendments but the Speaker makes the choice as to which amendments will be debated by the whole House of Commons.
The House can change what the Standing Committee has
passed and new amendments not considered by the Standing
Committee can be debated and decided upon.

Third reading of a bill This is the last chance MPs or Peers
get to vote on the bill as a whole. This stage is usually a
formality. Amendments can be put down and considered but
this is, on the whole, not welcomed.

Consideration of a Commons Bill by the Lords

A bill which has passed through all its stages in the House
of Commons does not automatically go up to the House of
Lords. It has to be introduced by a Peer. In the case of a
Government bill it will be introduced by a Minister sitting
in the Lords. In the case of a Private Member's Bill the

sponsor in the Commons must get a Peer to adopt the bill and take charge of its passage through the Lords. Each bill has to pass through all stages in both Houses before it becomes law.

As it goes through its various stages the bill may be considerably amended. Eventually, if it passes its third reading, it is sent back to the Commons as amended. These amendments may be accepted or rejected by the Commons or alterations proposed and the bill returned to the Lords. There is then one more chance of reaching agreement. When both Houses agree to the bill then it receives Royal Assent. Royal Assent is when the bill is taken to the Monarch for signature. This in practice is a formality since the reigning Monarch has given to Parliament the authority to make laws. Most bills include a clause which sets the time when it comes into operation. This is usually between twenty-eight days and three months after it has received Royal Assent. This may be longer if the new statute demands great revision to existing practices.

Bills which originate in the House of Lords

Many bills are introduced first in the Lords and generally follow the same procedure in reverse to that described for bills which are introduced in the Commons. In the case of a Government bill which is first introduced in the Lords, it will be considered first by Peers and will then be sent to the Commons. After MPs have completed consideration of the bill and have amended it, the bill will then be returned to the Lords who will either accept, amend or reject the Commons amendments. If there is a major disagreement between the two Houses then the Whips in both Houses will attempt to reach a compromise. Both the 1985 Shops Bill and the 1990 Human Fertilisation and Embryology Bill began their passage in the House of Lords.

Parliamentary questions

Any MP is entitled to ask questions of any Government Minister on the work of their Department, either as a written or an oral question. Written questions appear in the Order Paper each day and replies are printed in Hansard (the daily Parliamentary Report of its proceedings). There is no limit to the number or frequency of written questions — in any Parliamentary year about 40,000 questions are put down. Opportunities for oral questions are, however, more limited. At the beginning of each day, the House of Commons opens with Question Time. On Tuesdays and Thursdays the Prime Minister comes before the House for Questions and from Monday to Thursday various Ministers come before the House to answer questions from MPs. A ballot decides which MPs can ask oral questions on a particular day.

Select Committees

A Select Committee works as an investigation committee, scrutinising the work of a Government Department. These were established in 1979 and each examines the work of a particular Department. They can ask to see written evidence and question witnesses, which usually takes place in public. The Parties are represented on Select Committees in direct proportion to the number of seats they have in the House of Commons.

Private Members' Bills

The time available for debating issues raised by backbench MPs is very restricted. A ballot is held at the beginning of each session of Parliament to determine which Members will have the opportunity of introducing a bill on a subject of their choice. This is known as the 'Private Members' Ballot'. Members who wish to take a bill through Parliament put their names forward two days beforehand.

The ballot itself is a procedural matter. However, it sparks off great activity among many pressure groups — CARE included. They are constantly looking for a Member willing to take up a bill relating to their particular concern. Many members know what they would like to tackle long before the ballot actually occurs.

To succeed these Bills need Government assistance, with extra time being given to help the Bill along. Though about twenty members are drawn in the ballot, only those coming in the top five have real hope of success because of the limited time. A controversial bill is prone to be defeated by filibustering — or 'talking out' — unless the Government is prepared to give extra time and support to a Bill it wants to see through.

A Private Member's Bill provides a platform for public debate. There is much publicity through the coverage given to it by the media.

Your MP

To find out the name of your MP, phone the House of Commons Information Office on 071–219 4272.

The European Community

The European Community currently consists of twelve independent states: France, the Federal Republic of Germany, Italy, Belgium, the Netherlands and Luxembourg (the original members), the United Kingdom, the Republic of Ireland and Denmark (which joined in 1973), Greece (which joined in 1986) and Spain and Portugal (which joined in 1986). Together they have a population of over 320 million. The Community set a target date of the end of 1992 for the completion of the Single European Market — that is, the removal of all physical, technical and financial barriers to trade within the EC.

The Community works through a number of institutions, the main ones being the Commission, the Council of Ministers, the Parliament and the Court of Justice.

The Council of Ministers

The Council of Ministers is the most powerful Community institution and its principal decision-making body. It meets in various forms (eg Social Affairs, Agriculture, Environment) and is attended by the relevant national Ministers and senior officials. The Commission is usually represented in the Council, but does not have voting rights.

The Presidency of the Council of Ministers rotates among the Member States every six months. This role enables the country concerned to initiate and order priorities for the Council. The Council and its Committees are based in Brussels.

The European Commission

The Commission is by far the largest of the Community institutions. It employs 16,000 officials, most of whom are located in Brussels although some of the Commission's offices are in Luxembourg. There are also staff in Delegations and press and information offices in major cities throughout the world (see page 178 for UK addresses).

The Commission's most important role is to initiate legislative proposals which are, for the most part, considered by the European Parliament and on which the Council of Ministers decides. The Commission also has responsibility for implementing some policies (eg management of the Common Agricultural Policy) and applying certain aspects of EC law (eg competition policy).

It consists of seventeen Commissioners appointed by the governments of the Member States. These Commissioners share among themselves responsibility for about thirty Directorates-General (DGs) and Services which are concerned with the different aspects of Community policy, like government departments.

The European Parliament

The European Parliament debates policy issues and must be consulted about major Community decisions. It also has a substantial shared power with the Council of Ministers over the Community budget. The Parliament's legislative powers were increased under the Single European Act in 1987.

However, it remains essentially a consultative, rather than a law-making, body. It is concerned with influence, not power.

The European Parliament is a directly elected body (every five years) of 518 members — 81 from the UK. It is divided along political rather than national lines: for example, socialists of various nationalities sit together even though they may not vote similarly on all issues.

The Parliament's activities are based in three cities: its administration is in Luxembourg, full public (plenary) sessions are held for a week each month in Strasbourg and meetings of the specialist committees are held in Brussels.

The Court of Justice

The Court of Justice is based in Luxembourg. The Court hears cases brought by the Commission against governments for infringements of Community law; appeals by governments against decisions of the Commissions; appeals by individuals and cases brought by Community staff. It also gives preliminary rulings on cases referred by the courts of Member States.

The structure of the Court is rather unusual to anyone familiar with the English legal system. It is headed by thirteen judges, one from each Member State plus one appointed on a system of rotation. They are assisted by six Advocates General who prepare impartial submissions which cover the facts as well as the legal arguments.

Your MEP

To find out the name and address of your MEP, phone the European Parliament Information Office on 071–222 0411.

SECTION 3

PRACTICAL ADVICE

1   Getting Started

Forming a team

Once you get a few committed activists together, the greatest danger is that you will attempt too much too soon. Do remember that it takes time to develop a team, and certain stages are vital.

Firstly, at the initial meeting members must be made to feel welcome. They need to get to know each other, so that a team spirit develops, rather than a set purpose being imposed on the group. The tone should be both friendly and businesslike.

The next important stage is achieving some early success. If people are to remain committed to the team they need to feel that something useful is being done, and that they can help. So aim to do something practical fairly early on — even if it is only something small, such as getting leaflets distributed efficiently or raising funds.

Once an atmosphere of trust has been established, and the team has a good understanding of its basic aims, you can then consider your methods. If the team has grown, it is unlikely that the methods suitable for a small group will adapt to serve a larger one, so you need to agree on how decisions will be made, how differences will be handled, and how to make sure work gets done.

Finally, it is important to assess the group's usefulness by reviewing its progress regularly. Is it doing the job it set out to do? Is communication within the group improving? Are arguments resolved peaceably? Is trust being built up?

Once your team has been established, you can concentrate on getting other people's help. On the whole, people respond better if what you are talking about is

- clear — try to put things in as concrete and commonsense a way as possible;
- important — the problem may not be earth-shattering, but it must be worth acting on;
- practical — an idea should offer something for all members to do;
- possible — the group should not waste time on unachievable aims;
- manageable — time and cost are important factors and must not be ignored;
- enjoyable — you need to appeal to people's imaginations, because if you want them to continue their support they must enjoy it!

Campaigning groups will attract people with different talents and backgrounds. They will be most successful if a team can be built which allocates the right people to the right tasks.

Whatever the task you have decided on, the following points need consideration. First, you should not have too small a group involved: you will need a wide range of skills and opinions available, as well as just the right number of pairs of hands. Secondly, you need to have within the group a broad agreement on the aims of the task. Thirdly, everyone should share a readiness to work together, and an ability to work as a team rather than putting self first. Remember to include those who have direct practical experience rather than merely professional qualifications, although of course there may sometimes be a need for expert advice as well.

There are some people who always need to be handled with care. These include

- experts — they may mean well but they sometimes take over: you want advice, not a decision or an entire plan of action imposed on you;
- committee freaks — some people love sitting on committees and playing games with 'points of order' and the like;
- ego-trippers — people who put their own needs before those of the group are unlikely to be any real help;
- can't say no-ers — some people cannot refuse and end up with more work than they can handle: you need to watch how much people take on.

Meetings

Like most things, meetings don't just happen — they have to be planned. Whether they are full group meetings or just a gathering of a sub-committee, an agenda is vital. The first step is to list the important issues which need discussion, and then to consider the nature of each item: for instance, is it straightforward or controversial; is additional information required; is it a matter for information only? Then the chairman can assess how much time should be spent on each item, and which matters are most urgent, in case there is not sufficient time to deal with everything.

A typical agenda may look like this:

The next meeting of the Blanktown Christian Action Group will be held on . . . at . . . from 8 pm to 9.30 pm.

Agenda
1. Prayer.
2. Apologies for absence.
3. Minutes of last meeting.
4. Matters arising.
5. Officers' reports:
   a. Chairman
   b. Secretary (including correspondence)

c. Treasurer.
6. Special business (events, campaigns, etc.).
7. Any other business.
8. Prayer.

If possible, people should have the agenda and a copy of the previous meeting's minutes a week or so before the meeting, so they know what is to be discussed and can give some thought to the items before the meeting.

The minutes are a record of what happened at a meeting, and they can be very useful in saving time and argument. People's memories can play tricks on them, and members often find that they have very different ideas of what happened at a meeting, or what action they are supposed to be taking. Getting things written down accurately and promptly is important.

Minutes of a meeting of Barton Christian Action Group held at 21 Oxford Road, Barton on 5th February 1990.

Present: John Smith (Chairman), Susan Brown, Mary Jones, Simon Green, Jill Taylor, Mark Matthews. Apologies for absence: Bill Bailey.

Reading: Psalm 2

Minutes of the meeting held on 4th January 1990 were read and agreed.

Matters arising: there were no matters arising.

Correspondence: To Mr Berry, a local solicitor, asking that he visit to address the group about the legal position over Sunday trading, on a date to be arranged at his convenience.

Other business:
1. Embryology and abortion: The dossier prepared jointly by Mrs Norman (a midwife), Dr Pattison (a GP) and Mr Hodges (a solicitor) has now been sent to all Midshire MPs. The dossier was read by those present and warmly approved. There is an urgent need for all Christians to write to their MPs stressing the importance of giving careful thought to the issues involved. Copies of the dossier (price £1) are available from Mary.
2. Broadcasting: differing announcements have been made by various government speakers regarding the position of Christian broadcasting stations. As many letters as possible should be sent to the Prime Minister, calling for clarification on this issue.
3. John suggested that the group should complain to the council about the threatened closure of the Barton village school. This was agreed.
ACTION: Mary will write this letter and bring a copy to the next meeting.

The rest of the meeting was spent in prayer.

Next meeting: 5th April 1990 at 7.30 pm at 21 Oxford Road, Barton.

Example: minutes of a meeting.

Minutes should say where and when the meeting took place, who attended (with apologies for absence), and list each item on the agenda, together with a note of any decisions taken and names of those responsible for carrying them out. They should be an accurate account of the proceedings, but should be kept as brief as possible: it is not necessary to record every speech and argument, but relevant comments and opinions should be noted. It is important to use the exact wording of motions and proposals, and to give the details of decisions taken.

All minutes should:

- be short and to the point;
- follow the same headings and numbers as the agenda;
- have decisions clearly marked 'AGREED';
- have an 'action column' for easy reference;
- be fair and honest.

The 'action column' alongside the details of decisions can show the initials of the members who are going to implement them. This saves confusion about who is supposed to be doing what. If the minutes of one meeting are circulated with the agenda for the next one, all members have a chance to consider them and recall any 'matters arising'. They are also prompted to fulfil any responsibilities in time for the next meeting. (See the example on pages 100–101.)

The actual conduct of the meeting depends greatly on what its aims are: it may be just for information or the review of an action, or there may be decisions to be taken. Making collective decisions can be difficult when there are many points of view to be heard. However, a variety of opinion usually makes for a better final decision, because if you can agree you will have pooled more information and have more people involved. This last point is important: making decisions means acting on the result.

There are several stages in making a decision.

- First agree on what method you will use — majority votes, consensus or delegation.
- Understand the problem fully — spend time clarifying details.
- Find out what information you need and make sure

everyone has it — the better the quality of your information, the better your decision.

- List all the possible solutions to the problem and ensure you are all fully informed about each; then look at the arguments for and against each course of action.
- When you have made the decision, choose people to carry out the specific action.
- Review the action — this is often forgotten! You can learn a lot by looking back and seeing how things work out in practice.

A good decision is one made at the right time by the right people; one which fits the facts and the resources available; one which is accepted by everyone; and is followed by action. This is a useful checklist for reviewing your activities!

Finance

Once you are writing letters and buying newspapers, a certain level of finance will become necessary: stationery, postage and telephone bills are expensive, and the burden should not fall on one or two members alone. Some groups have official membership fees, others ask for donations from individuals or supporting churches, others run fund-raising events. It is important not to be embarrassed about the financial needs of the group. However, once people are giving you money for whatever reason, you owe it to them to be businesslike in your dealings with it. It's a great temptation at first to shoulder the costs of stamps and photocopying alone, until you realise just how much that is going to cost you. Then it may seem better to take small amounts out of 'petty cash' so as to avoid having to keep proper records: but this is not a good idea either, as it's hard to keep track of what you have spent, or to make estimates of what funds you may need in the future. In particular, you may run a campaign for which it is possible to obtain a grant from the council or a trust fund: in that case, you will almost certainly have to produce accounts or estimates of expenses.

There is no mystique about keeping accounts: you simply have to be methodical. First of all, buy two small cash books: one is for recording your petty cash, the other for your main accounts. Open each to the first double page and on the left-hand page write 'Incoming money', and on the right-hand page write 'Outgoing money'. Each time you receive some money you record the date, the source (such as gift, collection or grant), and the exact amount on the left-hand page. At the same time you should buy a receipt book with duplicate pages, and write a receipt for the person giving you the money. That way the donor has a record, and you have a double record: the duplicate page of the receipt book and your account book.

Each time some money is spent you record the date, the purpose and the exact amount. The receipt you are given in the shop should be kept in an envelope marked 'receipts', so that again you have a double record which can be checked. Sometimes you will have to record in your 'outgoing money' column that you have transferred some money to petty cash; this sum will then appear as 'incoming money' in the petty cash book. (See below.)

Date	Incoming money	£ p	Date	Outgoing money	£ p
1.2.90	Collection	25.30	1.2.90	Petty cash	25.30
4.3.90	Donation from	50.00	6.3.90	Stationery	15.00
	Trinity Church		7.4.90	Mrs Brown (paper)	10.00
			9.5.90	Hire of hall	12.00
			9.5.90	Petty cash	5.00

Example: an account book.

Date	Incoming money £	p	Date	Outgoing money £	p
1.2.90	Collection	25.30	3.2.90	Stamps	5.00
9.5.90	Petty cash	5.00	4.3.90	Envelopes	2.50
			4.4.90	Photocopying	3.50
			5.5.90	Photocopying	3.50
			6.5.90	Stationery	10.79

Example: a petty cash book.

You will probably want to open a bank account for your group once you have got beyond the petty cash stage; the bank will explain to you how to do this. You usually need two officials to open the account and to sign any cheques; you may be able to persuade a friendly bank manager to waive bank charges for a good cause.

At the end of the year you can go over your accounts and check that the amounts of money all add up correctly. This will probably be enough for your members, but if you receive any grant aid you may be asked for audited accounts; you need to find an accountant to check your accounts and write a statement confirming that they are correct. Don't forget that financial records must be kept for at least seven years in case anyone wishes to see the books, even if your group stops meeting or your campaign is over.

Filing

Decide early on how you will deal with paperwork and keep records, as it can easily mount up and be a source of discouragement. You don't need to go to the extent of purchasing a huge filing system — just buy two box-files and several plastic folders. A filing system allowing easy retrieval will greatly add to your efficiency and effectiveness.

Making plans

No two campaigns are the same, but the elements of a successful campaign probably include:

- a clear idea of what you want to achieve;
- setting realistic objectives;
- a good knowledge of your targets;
- determination and persistence;
- careful organisation;
- getting access to resources;
- using a variety of tactics;
- making allies;
- doing the unexpected;
- keeping the initiative;
- being positive.

One of the ironies of politics is that the time when you are most likely to succeed is the time when you are least likely to act — perhaps because you have not realised the importance of an issue, or because you are not yet sufficiently organised. You need to be an active group before issues surface, so that you are ready with contacts and resources when the time is right.

You can do this by building up goodwill: get the respect of decision-makers as a voice to be listened to, make links with possible allies, and build up a public image that people find sympathetic. You also need to maintain your organisation, by keeping your members involved and active, so that people know their jobs: they need to have the resources (cash, access to printing, etc.) ready to start a campaign. Watch developments constantly, looking out for indicators of public opinion and what decision-makers are thinking. Do not wait for firm statements or for the story to break in the press before you start to act.

Understanding issues

You should know as much as possible about the subject of your campaign: what has happened in the past, and why has the issue become important now? What are the facts, the needs, and who has an interest in it? What are the possible solutions, what would be the results of each possibility, and which do you prefer? It is especially important to keep in touch with the thinking of the whole group — usually there is an active core to any group, and it is important that they should not be campaigning for different aims from those of the majority of members.

Before you begin to plan any action, it is essential that you know who holds the authority in your area: who takes decisions on the issue? Who influences the decision-makers? What will make them see matters your way? You should take special note of newspapers and the media — they can have enormous influence on public opinion, and it is public opinion (and therefore potential votes) which influences politicians.

It will be useful for your group to begin building up a library of information such as names, addresses and telephone numbers for the following:

- all members (a telephone chain can save time and money when urgent messages have to be passed on to everyone);
- all local churches and their ministers (and their level of interest and support);
- all local para-church organisations (and their level of interest and support);
- other useful Christian and informative organisations (be on their mailing lists);
- local facilities and services (the Council and the library are good resources);
- local Christian Unions in schools, colleges, hospitals, etc;
- all local councillors;
- your constituency MP (and his or her views on issues of Christian concern);

- your MEP;
- local branches of political parties;
- members of a prayer chain, which works rather like the telephone chain to pass on local and national needs;
- other resources: where to obtain particular information, books, leaflets, etc.;
- local newspapers and the media — one member should be responsible for keeping press cuttings, and another for contacting the media and making statements to be reported.

Strategy

Advance planning is often the key to success: a campaign which is poorly planned and badly organised is doomed to failure from the start. You need a clear idea of what you intend to achieve, and of the chances of success. You may have to determine priorities and decide to concentrate your attention and resources on only a few activities.

There are a number of questions which should be asked right at the beginning.

- How long will the campaign run for?
- What resources do we have?
- How can we best use the resources?
- What are our strongest arguments?
- How can we best present them?
- What weaknesses are there in our case?
- How can we best deal with them?
- What tactics should we use to ensure success?
- How do we respond to the campaign of our opponents?

In the case of a community campaign, you need to ask whether you already have public opinion on your side, or whether you need to start by convincing people of your case. If so, all the information in support of your case needs to be readily available — perhaps you need a preliminary time of activity to collect that information and present it in a

Cheshire County Council decided to write to all news-agents in their area asking them to take a 'responsible attitude' towards the display of pornographic magazines. The decision came shortly after a widely publicised campaign run by the Tatton CARE group, which found that 89% of local women interviewed wanted pornography removed from public display.

striking form. Local authorities will respond to well-organised campaigns.

Although advance planning is important, you should avoid too rigid a plan: you may need to adapt to changing circumstances as time goes on, and amend your strategy in the light of new information and developments. Ideally you should agree a basic plan at the outset, but ensure that your organisation is sufficiently flexible to allow you to vary the details as the campaign progresses.

Some people have a flair for campaigning and are bold and imaginative when deciding their strategy; others prefer a more cautious approach. Make use of the strengths of your group and be aware of weaknesses. You don't have to win every battle to win the war!

Often it is better to take a positive initiative rather than to complain when your group does not like something that is happening locally. For example, a CARE group in north-east Scotland was concerned about teaching materials being used in the local primary school. Instead of making a formal complaint they approached a Christian publisher who agreed that if the group raised £100, they would give £200 worth of quality educational materials with a Christian basis to the local school. This initiative fostered excellent relationships with the school and secured very good publicity in the local paper.

Choose your methods

As with deciding your campaign strategy, you need to consider local circumstances and your own resources when choosing your techniques: what is right for one campaign may be wrong for another. Nevertheless, you should cast your net as wide as possible: variety keeps the public interested, as well as your members.

- Canvassing — to obtain opinions and to explain your case — can be carried out door-to-door or in public places (shopping centres, bus terminals, etc.).
- Petitions can be used to back up your case: ask local shops and businesses to display petition forms, or get local interest groups to circulate their members. Ensure you get sufficient response for the petition to be credible and stand a chance of influencing the decision-makers. Set a deadline by which the forms must be returned to the organiser, and allow a couple of days for latecomers. There is a special format for a petition which is to be presented to Parliament by an MP on behalf of a group of his constituents. Ask for the leaflet about petitions from the Clerk of Public Petitions in the Journal Office of the House of Commons, Westminister, London SW1A 0AA.
- Surveys, like petitions and canvassing, can be conducted door-to-door or in public areas. They usually ask questions — such as whether people support the granting of a licence to a sex shop or abortion clinic. You may wish to distribute survey forms in advance, so that people have a chance to complete them before you return to collect them, or you may fill in the form yourself as you interview individuals. Alternatively you may decide not to use a form but to record replies informally on a clipboard.
- Reports, based on the replies to your canvassing and surveys, may form a submission to the council, or be of use in planning your future strategy. Ensure that the style of the report is appropriate for the people who will be

reading it. If the report is for the general public it should be brief and succinct; if it is for council officials or a committee it should include more detail: you need to convince them that you have a sound grasp of statistics and know what you are talking about. (For more detail, see 'Reports', p. 153.)

- Leaflets and newsletters can be used to explain what your campaign is about, and to keep people informed of how it is progressing. Ensure that the style is lively and interesting, and that the content is suitable for the readership.

- Meetings and rallies can be worthwhile when the issue is a 'hot' one, attracting a lot of public interest. Make sure they are properly advertised and organised, and that the press is fully informed. You must have a clear aim and know what you hope to achieve through the meeting: it should be relevant to local needs and concerns. (See 'Public meetings', p. 146.)

- Pickets, lobbies and demonstrations can be effective if timed to coincide, for instance, with councillors arriving for a meeting. Demonstrations should always be peaceful. Notify the press and arrange a good visual effect with placards containing suitable slogans, etc.

- Stickers and posters can emphasise a point or draw attention to a problem: choose a suitable slogan. Remember that flyposting is illegal, and you have to obtain the site owner's consent to display a board or sign.

- Lobbies of councillors or officials can be effective. Personal approaches from individual electors often carry far more weight than protest petitions, particularly if the individuals have a vote in the area the councillor represents. Arrange for people to phone or write to every member of the planning committee before a meeting: circulate lists of addresses and phone numbers, or perhaps display a councillor's work phone number as parents bring their children to school in the morning, and his home phone number as they come to collect them in the afternoon. Advertise a different councillor or officer each day.

- Press publicity is free publicity, and it is invaluable. Make a point of finding out which reporters are most sympathetic to good campaigning stories, and keep them informed. Be aware of any new angles on each story to maintain their interest. (See 'Handling the Media' p. 128.)
- Street theatre is a novel way of conveying a point. Have a short story-line which, acted out, explains what the problem is and how you want it tackled. Novel ways of presenting your case may win you new interest and support.

There are many other possibilities, of course, and the only limits are your imagination and resources. You should be always on the lookout for new ideas — simply using the same old literature and press releases time after time is not good enough. People will not support you if they are bored, or have seen it all before! You might consider holding a 'brain-storming' session for your key activists, to exchange ideas on how to improve your organisation and communications. If you have any members with special expertise, such as graphic designers, journalists or PR consultants, use them to the full.

Don't get caught in the trap of preaching to the converted: be ready to contact people wherever you can find them. Clubs and societies may be used to put over your message in a variety of ways, but don't forget their notice boards. You may be allowed to display a card giving details of your activities and contact person. Notice boards outside shops and Post Offices are also worthy of attention. Advertising there is usually extremely cheap, and enormous numbers of people read them. Check the details for your area. Yellow Pages and local directories are often the first places people look for information. Is your group listed, and are the details up to date? Remember, too, that fetes, carnivals and other local events are attended by large numbers of people — always book an information stall and make it look interesting.

Opposition

No guide to campaigning would be complete without consideration of what your opponents are doing. A good campaigner is always aware of what the rivals are doing, and whether their activities are a challenge. If they are, you may need to consider responding to the opposition.

When your opponents produce a newsletter or a press release, or launch a campaign, or do anything which may create support for their message and decrease support for yours, three questions should be asked:

- Is the opposition a threat?
- Should we respond, and how?
- What effect will a response have on public opinion — on our supporters — on the opposition?

For example, it may be that an opposition newsletter is so abysmal that it is best ignored. Responding to it may only give it some credibility and encourage the opposition to continue. However, if their efforts are worth taking seriously and are likely to have any effect, then a response may be necessary.

Before deciding on any action, consider such things as whether the opposition newsletter is likely to be a 'one-off' or the first of a series. Is it targeted to one particular constituency? Has one individual produced it, or is the whole opposition playing you at your own game? Is it a challenge, now or in the future, and how can you best respond?

If opponents begin campaigning in one of your constituencies and start producing competent local newsletters, consider increasing your own output with special local issues, press releases, survey leaflets, petitions — more than they can cope with. At the same time, point out any inaccuracies, mistakes, dubious statements etc in the opposition leaflet. A polite and positive approach is best: say what a pity it is that their leaflet was so riddled with inaccuracies or personal attacks that they have done themselves a disservice.

Make it quite clear to your opponents that their efforts have stirred up such a volume of Christian activity that it is really not in their interest to continue. Demonstrate that anything they can do, you can do better: make your newsletter more attractive and more frequent than theirs, your overall approach more effective.

Always consider carefully the effect on the public: do a survey to find out which newsletters they remember best, and why; find out what is most likely to persuade them to change their support. Learn how to improve your performance.

Consider also the effect of your response on your opponents. Will it encourage or discourage them? Will it persuade them to widen or narrow the range of their activities? Always think things through: what would you like your opponents to do, and how can you persuade them to do just that?

2 *Prayer*

At the heart of the Christian life is the ministry of prayer. Without deep intercessory prayer, nothing can be achieved, and all the activities outlined in this book depend upon this firm foundation. It is essential that any groups or individuals embarking upon such activities should first seek the will of God in deciding their course of action and following it through.

A dedication to regular and listening prayer constantly refines our motives and gives us fresh vision for the tasks ahead. The apostle Paul commands us to 'pray in the Spirit at all times', and groups will find their work bearing fruit only if this is a reality in their corporate life as a group and as individuals.

Whatever activities we become involved in, the work is God's, and not our own. He is the commander of the battle against evil and injustice, and we are obeying his will.

> Finally, be strong in the Lord and in his mighty power. Put on the full armour of God so that you can take your stand against the devil's schemes. For our struggle is not against flesh and blood, but against the rulers, against the authorities, against the powers of this dark world and against the spiritual forces of evil in the heavenly realms . . . pray in the Spirit on all occasions with all kinds of prayers and requests. With this in mind, be alert and always keep on praying for the saints (Eph 6:10–12,18).

First steps in prayer

The first step is to make a list of Christians whom God has strategically placed in positions of authority and influence. Find out who they are and how they most need help. God has done remarkable things through his people being in the right place at the right time: Joseph, Daniel and Esther were all clearly in the minority, but they were used by God to do his will. We need men and women in positions of influence to accomplish similar miracles today.

We may be led to pray that God will remove ungodly men and women from office in order to prevent the promotion of injustice, corruption and atheistic policies — and this may mean praying against the political party we favour. On the other hand, we may ask God to change someone's attitude rather than remove them. The account of Jonah shows us how first the King of Nineveh and then the whole population changed; they turned away from their sin and fasted and prayed when they heard God's warning of judgement on the city.

Sometimes we need to look beyond the individuals who seem to be opposed to God's will: Ephesians 6:12 teaches us about the devil's activity, and that an unseen struggle of a different nature is also going on. As we pray we must remember these powerful spiritual forces of evil, which may be manipulating individuals and groups. A group of Christians recently were interceding for the City of London; they became increasingly convinced that there were evil spirits of greed and unrighteousness influencing the trade and business there. They prayed against these forces and the grip they held on institutions. Subsequently various companies and individuals have been exposed for their corrupt business dealings and their abuse of power.

If as the Body of Jesus Christ we fail to take seriously this spiritual dimension, we will fail to make an effective impression on our nation's problems. But we need to take care: it is vital to be balanced and biblical when we examine these issues and begin to pray accordingly.

The ministry of prayer is both challenging and exciting. We need the support of one another, sensitivity, wisdom, boldness, patience, and the authority given to us by God. We must also remember that prayer should be backed up by a willingness to act, to present positive alternatives to society.

Suggestions

Christians who are praying for those in authority may like to consider these suggestions.

- Be committed — try to commit yourself to pray on a regular basis. Regard this as a helpful discipline rather than a legal bondage!
- Be together — try to join with others to pray rather than doing it alone. As prayer-group members grow to love and trust one another, so spiritual depth and faith increase.
- Be informed — reliable newspapers, programmes and Christian publications like CARE's prayer guide can keep you up to date and provide valuable insights. Where possible, pray for real people and situations rather than abstract concepts. Appoint a co-ordinator to collect names and information that will add to your prayers.
- Be local — try to apply any general prayer topics to the specific situations locally. Thousands may be praying for the national education system: who is praying for the Head Teacher of the school round the corner?
- Be Bible-centred — always pray according to scriptural principles, teaching and promises. Ask God to counsel, teach and show you what to pray and how to go about it.
- Be prepared — when you feel equipped and confident, you can move on from prayer requests, to spiritual warfare against the devil's grip on people and institutions.

- Be safe — beware of 'doing it alone'. Ask a Christian leader whom you respect to keep a watching brief as your prayer ministry develops. Consider linking with local or national prayer fellowships. Be open to guidance and help to keep balanced, outward-looking, and full of faith as you pray.

Finally, encourage others to join you and pray for the nation and for those in authority: your country needs your prayers!

CARE believes in the power of God to change lives and situations; we are in a spiritual battle and therefore see prayer as an essential part of every programme of action. The CARE Prayerline (071 233 0976) is updated regularly, and a quarterly Prayer Guide is distributed.

3 Lobbying

This is a way of trying to influence people who have power so that they will support your ideas and plans. It can be used to affect a decision which is about to be made by a council, a company, a union, etc, or it may simply be a means of making someone aware of your group and its thinking, to prepare for future campaigns. Because it involves personal contact, it can be a useful way of getting decision-makers to say where they stand on an issue, and it may also produce useful results.

The word 'lobbying' is often used to mean talking to people directly, rather than exchanging letters in the press. It is basically a conversation, and as such it has all the strengths and weaknesses of informal contact. On the one hand it reminds the decision-makers that issues are about real people, and may show the strength of feeling on a subject far more effectively than letter-writing. It is also more flexible: you ask a question and have a reasonable chance of insisting on an immediate response.

On the other hand, there may be unexpected difficulties. Lobbying usually takes place on the councillor's or official's territory — you go to see them — and so they are likely to have more control over what happens than you. The personal contact involves the risk that the individual may take a personal dislike to you, which may colour his attitude to your case. You may find yourself drawn into their way of working,

119

and find yourself committed to points which you would not have agreed to if you had time to think (as you would with letter-writing). And of course, as with any conversation, it is very easy to be sidetracked from your issues into talking about something entirely different.

In spite of these dangers, lobbying is often very worth while. Letters and reports will inform the decision-makers about the facts; your personal visit can convey your feelings — especially your determination to achieve your purpose. A personal conversation can also cover matters which are confidential and cannot be written down and made public — for instance, explaining why it may be in someone's interest to support a particular issue. Remember that it may be helpful to lobby some people before a campaign starts, and get their commitment for the future.

When planning a lobby it is important to know whom you are meeting: for instance, if you are visiting a local councillor, do a little research and find out what committees he is on, what his attitude has been to similar issues, what his job is, and so on. Think carefully about location. If you can get people onto your home ground it will be an advantage. Better still, try to persuade your target to meet you at the site of the problem (if it is a visible one) — if you are campaigning against the sex shop next door to your children's school, try to get the councillor to the school. Not only does this convey first-hand experience of the situation, but it can also make a good news story.

Issue a press release and try to get an item in the newspaper before your meeting : this has the advantage of doubling the press coverage (before and after) and of putting the other person on the spot. If an item has already appeared in the paper or on local radio, the issue becomes one of public importance, and most politicians or local groups will want to be seen to be doing something. Timing can be important, and you should always lobby early enough to make your efforts worthwhile, and give your target group time to discuss your suggestions. On the other hand, lobbying immediately before an important meeting can sometimes be successful.

Think about the size of your delegation. If an individual knows a councillor well, then a personal approach may work, although your message may not get across with as much force as when two or more people arrive together. It is usually better to lobby in a group — it means you can give one another support and let the councillor know that there is a number of people with strong feelings on the matter. If you do go as a group, make sure that everyone knows who is doing what. Have a list of questions prepared, and share them out, so that different members take responsibility for ensuring that different questions get answered.

Make sure that everyone is fully briefed and informed, and have your facts straight — nothing looks worse than someone getting some simple fact wrong. Have suitable material on hand to support your case, and a written statement which you can leave behind so that the councillor has a record of what you think about the issues. If you have the chance to prepare a proper presentation, take along slides and visual aids: a display of pictures will make your case more vividly, and also remind you of some of the points you wish to make.

Think about how you present yourselves — remember that appearances can be very important. You are there to win friends and influence people, so be friendly, fair and firm; if you are too forceful the person you are lobbying may become hostile.

Appoint one of your number to take notes of what is said at the meeting so that you have a record, and to send a letter afterwards outlining what you understand to have been said and promised. Issue a press statement afterwards, as well, to keep up the media interest. Take care if a joint statement is suggested, as you will want the wording to reflect your position. In particular, watch out for the headline — is it fair to your point of view? — the first line — does it say clearly that this is a joint statement? — the text — are all your points listed? — and the contact number for further details — is your member's number listed?

Writing to the Government and your MP

CARE are often asked for advice on writing to MPs. To help you, here is a simple guide to writing letters to those in Government and to your MP.

Why write?

Writing a letter, is without doubt, the most effective way of expressing your thoughts, opinions and questions to your MP. It is the best method of official communication. In turn, MPs are always keen to hear constituents' views. An MP, as an elected representative, wants and needs to hear views from his constituents, so that he can respond to their concerns. An MP's postbag is his most immediate source of knowledge of the burning issues within the constituency. And it only takes a few well-written letters to convey strong feeling from local people. Letter writing has a two-way effect between the MP and the constituency. Don't forget to thank your MP for voting for a bill you wanted him to support. Also it is good to encourage MPs — assure them you are praying for them. They need your support.

How to write

Handwritten or typed personal letters are by far the best way to communicate strongly held views to your MP. If you are writing by hand, make sure your writing is legible. Bad handwriting is a wasted letter since busy MPs do not have the time to decipher obscure hieroglyphics!

Always address your MP personally and sign the letter personally. Send letters by first class post. Generally avoid circulars or pre-printed letters which only require a signature and address. At best these will only be given a cursory glance and at worst disregarded altogether.

Presentation of a letter is also very important. Letters should preferably be no more than one side of A4 in length. The points you want to make should be briefly stated and clearly identifiable. There is no need to write at length on every point you make.

However, if you feel you need to explain a point further and include more factual detail, then it is best to write a separate detailed paper using a personal letter as a covering note which should explain the main points of the paper. MPs generally do not have the time to read reams of paper. This type of approach may be useful if a constituent has particular or professional interest in the subject in question and can offer the MP specialised information which may help him to reach a more informed decision (eg a gynaecologist writing about an abortion bill may well wish to use this approach). In general, though, a letter is sufficient.

Letter writing campaigns are important and effective. However, as stated above, avoid pre-printed letters. If you are asking people to write on an issue make sure you, and they, have sufficient information to write an informed letter. Information on the basic points and issues can always be conveyed in a simple leaflet.

Where to write

Writing to your MP Always write to your MP at the House of Commons, Westminster, London, SW1A 0AA. To find out the name of your MP, phone the House of Commons Information Office on 071–219 4272.

Writing to Government Departments It is often important and useful to write to Government Departments and the Secretary of State to make your views known on an issue for which their department is responsible. This is a good way of expressing a body of opinion to the Government. The best way of channelling an opinion through to Government is to ask your MP to raise a particular issue or concern with the relevant Government Minister. All you need to do is write to your MP asking him to raise a question on Government policy with the relevant Minister. The MP will then inform you when he receives a reply.

Writing to the Prime Minister   This is a useful channel for expressing an opinion rather than raising a question. Letters received at Downing Street are noted and then often passed to the relevant Government Department for reply. So don't be surprised (or disappointed) if you don't get a reply from the Prime Minister! Letters should be addressed to the Prime Minister at 10 Downing Street, London, SW1.

When your MP is a Government Minister

We are often asked, 'What is the point of writing to my MP when he is a Member of the Government?'

The means by which Government Ministers are constrained is known as 'collective responsibility'. That is, those on the Government 'pay-roll' vote together on Government Bills unless there is a free vote. But it is important to make your views known to your MP, whatever his position is. Even though a Minister may not vote the way you would like, if there is a sufficient body of opinion reflecting your position in his constituency then this will probably be made known, formally or informally, to the highest levels of Government. MPs, whether part of the Government or not, are always sensitive to the strength of constituency feeling. Views on the advisability of any measure will always be taken into account. One of the best ways of judging this, for any MP, is through his post bag.

Letter writing, far from being an onerous task, is often enjoyable and even exciting. Try once and then your confidence will increase. With adequate information, letter writing means you enter into the to-and-fro of opinion and debate which is a basic right in a democratic society and you are also using this avenue to raise a Christian voice to our legislators. The more people who write letters the better!

Meeting your MP

The best time to meet your MP will be during his surgery — a period of time set aside for meeting constituents and listening to their views and problems. Some constituents will be seeking practical help with housing problems, for example, and others will be expressing their opinions on topical issues and trying to influence the way their MP will vote in Parliament.

Surgeries are usually held in the MP's constituency. The local library, Citizen's Advice Bureau, or the local political party association office, will know where and when the surgery is held and how to make an appointment.

Preparation for the meeting

- Decide whether you are going to see the MP on your own, or as part of a delegation. Small groups of five people or less are more imposing than a single visitor, and show the wide support for a point of view. Lobbying in groups means that you will give each other valuable support. Larger groups are more difficult to organise.

  Remember to book the meeting as soon as possible as surgery time is limited, and check how long you will have with the MP. If you are going to meet your MP alone follow all the suggestions as for a group but you must be able to argue your case powerfully and cogently.
- Arrange a preparation meeting for the delegation. Decide first what you want to achieve through the meeting with the MP and how you are going to achieve it. Appoint a leading spokesperson or chairman who will take charge of the discussion. It is also important to have a secretary who will take notes.
- Make a list of the matters you want answers to and the

points you want to cover. It is easy to get side-tracked by professional politicians on to matters they want to talk about but you do not! Careful preparation beforehand will give you confidence.

- Get your facts straight and your questions ready. MPs want to know facts and nothing looks worse then getting simple facts wrong. Do your homework. Briefing material on all of CARE's concerns is available from headquarters and should be used extensively.
- Organise yourselves. Work out what points need to be made and by whom. Decide who is best equipped to argue the various aspects of a case. Make sure they are a good spokesperson. Remember it is better to make a few points well than try to get too many in and make them badly. Practise together and try to anticipate the responses from the MP and how you can respond.
- Know your MP's background. Find out how he has voted in the past on the issue or related matters. What committees is he a member of? What was his job before becoming an MP? Does he have any special interest he champions in Parliament? A good source for this information is Dod's Parliamentary Companion, which should be stocked by most good reference libraries.

Conducting the meeting

Always be polite, receptive and friendly but firm. It is never productive to be rude, aggressive and hostile as this only demeans the cause for which you are fighting. This attitude will certainly antagonise the MP. Never threaten or accuse your MP. Make these points clear to your delegation before the meeting. If anyone does become aggressive towards the MP, the chairman should immediately intervene. However, if the MP tries to evade your questions, then politely but firmly repeat them until you get answers. Be disciplined as a group. Try not to let the MP dictate the direction of the conversation.

Try to get your MP to say how he intends to vote. You are only interested in his personal feelings as they influence how he will vote in Parliament.

Take notes of the key points of the meeting so that you have a record of what has been said.

Leave your MP with any relevant written material to support what you have discussed.

Before you leave, thank the MP for giving you his time and for what he does in and for the constituency.

4 Handling the Media

Local newspapers, radio and television can provide your group with a great deal of free publicity; however, contrary to general opinion, not all publicity is good publicity. A newspaper story on your local campaign may well be of enormous assistance to you, but if it is slanted in the wrong way, it may prove to be a hindrance. The media will never be under your control — their job is to report news and sell newspapers, not act as your mouthpiece. However, you can do a great deal to ensure that most reports of your activities are accurate and favourable.

Making news

Press publicity is important: it can help you to educate people about local issues, it can get you members and helpers, put pressure on decision-makers, and attract people to the events you organise. On the other hand, some news is bad news. The things you do and the way in which they get reported may make you unpopular with the very people you are trying to influence. You therefore need to be very careful about the way you use the press, and the way the press uses you. A good first step is to appoint a press officer for your group.

The press officer can co-ordinate all the publicity for your group, and be the person whose name is known to journalists when they want a story. The officer should be good at talking to people, able to write in clear English, and able to recognise the types of stories or angles that are newsworthy. The press officer should also

- know what the group wants to achieve and how they intend to do it — so that when the right moment comes the story is ready;
- know the market — the different styles of the papers and programmes, special interests and so on;
- know which papers people read and which programmes they listen to — local councillors usually read the local weekly papers carefully and listen to early morning radio shows;
- make himself known to reporters — friendly relations encourage the press to treat you favourably, so it is helpful to know your reporters personally.

Timing is important: you must keep an eye on the press and be aware of the best moment to 'break' your story. The more topical the story, the greater the prominence it is likely to get. A useful ploy is to try to connect up your message with other events: for instance, if you are campaigning for better facilities for the disabled you could make a link with news coverage of sports for the disabled ('You need to be an athlete to get up the steps to the Post Office'). However, don't be tempted to get your stories into the press too early: bear in mind the timing of the rest of the campaign.

The press works to a very strict timetable, and stories need to be in on time to get a reasonable coverage. A rough guide to deadlines is as follows:

- weekly newspapers: 2–3 days before publication (if the paper is due out on Friday, the news should be in on Monday or Tuesday);
- morning papers: up to 9 pm the evening before, but early afternoon is better;
- evening papers: 11 am for the same day;

- local radio: for news programmes, about an hour before the broadcast;
- weekly magazines: at least 2–3 days before publication (a week to be safe);
- monthly magazines: at least two weeks ahead of publication.

These deadlines apply to news items you supply. If you want to get a reporter to cover an event it is vital to give plenty of notice (up to three weeks). A major reason for lack of press coverage is failure to give sufficient notice.

There are three basic ways of getting press coverage: talking to journalists, issuing press releases, and writing letters to the editor. Talking to journalists may seem to be the simplest way, but like anything else it requires careful forethought. You must always have a clear idea of what you want to say, and try to avoid saying anything you don't mean. There are several danger areas, such as being rushed. If you are unsure about something, call back later with the accurate information — don't be pressured into saying something you think may be wrong. Next, try to picture how your words will be used; if you have nothing to say, or if you are denying something, be positive and give an explanation. Watch out for summaries: a common technique used by journalists is to put a long question which needs only 'yes' or 'no' for answer. You may be agreeing to something which you did not notice. Remember, too, that most people talk more on the telephone than face to face — it is easy to say more than you meant to. If you forget something, or have further information or news, telephone the reporter back; it is worth while if the points are important. If the paper has specialist reporters, try to get the name of the individual concerned, and remember to make a note of the conversation afterwards.

Always keep a record of what the press or radio did with your story, checking whether it was fair and got across the points you wanted. If it did not, then do something about it — get a follow-up story to set the record straight. Try also to check whether there has been any reaction to the story.

Press releases

Press releases can provide background information and details for a campaign, give notice of a coming event, report an event, meeting or speech, or be the basis for an interview. The first question to ask is whether your release is news — does it have the human interest or novelty that journalists like? If not, then do something about it. For instance, rather than saying that you disagree with the granting of a sex shop licence, stress the danger of pornography for the community and the family. Make the style of your press release interesting and imaginative, and then it is more likely to be used.

Every press release should include five Ws:

> What is happening.
> Who is doing it.
> Where it is taking place.
> When it is taking place.
> Why it is taking place.

Use simple, short sentences, avoid jargon and abbreviations, and make your news easy to read. (See the example in 'Resources'.)

If you want your copy to be published regularly you must establish yourself as a reliable source: take great care over facts, especially names and initials, and never say anything you do not mean or are unable to prove. Put your facts in descending order of importance (major points first).

Always try to use a quote: it will make your story come alive because it personalises the statement. It can also be a way of including opinions as well as facts. The sentence

> The local CARE group is writing to complain about the extra-ordinary amount of money the local Health Authority is spending on new abortion clinics

sounds wrong — it has too much opinion where we expect facts. A good change would be:

> Local CARE campaigners are complaining about the amount of money the local Health Authority is spending on new abortion facilities. 'We don't need more abortion clinics — the money would be better spent in helping single parents.'

This sounds more positive and offers an alternative use for the money.

When preparing your press release you should consider the following checklist.

- Length. Try to keep to one side of A4 paper only; if the release has to be longer, number the pages in the top right hand corner, and make sure they are all stapled firmly together.
- Headed paper. Make sure the journalists know where the release is coming from; if you don't have headed paper, print the name of your group clearly at the top.
- Date. Always put the date when the press release was issued.
- Embargo. This tells the press when the story can be published, and means that you can send the story to the press well before you want it published. An embargo is often used for surprise events, demonstrations, and so on, which need news coverage without losing the surprise element. On the whole you should avoid embargoes unless absolutely necessary; if you have to use one, make the reason clear.
- Headlines. A headline should be simple and give an idea of the content — a shortened form of the first sentence will do. Type it in capitals and leave plenty of space around it for the editor to write instructions on.
- First paragraph. This is crucial as it determines whether the reader reads on or not. Never make it longer than two sentences: the first should contain four of the Ws — who,

what, when and where. Then you can go on to why. A story will be a winner if the action taken (eg Christian Action Group blocks Children's Home closure) dramatises the issue (eg the high proportion of homeless children in the area).

- Text. Keep the rest of the text short and easy to read, and start each paragraph a couple of line spaces down from the previous one. Keep using the five Ws! At the end, write ENDS.

Press Release available for immediate publication 13th October 1989

WOMEN'S ATTITUDES TO SOFT PORN IN CONGLETON

Women from Christian Action, Congleton, will be conducting a survey next week on the attitudes of local women to the sale of 'soft porn' magazines by newsagents.

The survey will take place during the week commencing the 21st October in the main shopping areas of Congleton. Women will be asked their opinion on the sale of 'soft' pornography and whether they think its widespread availability encourages assaults on women.

Paul Knight, co-ordinator of Christian Action, said: 'We have contacted ten newsagents in the town centre and advised them of our proposed action, expressing our concern about these magazines. We feel confident that women from all walks of life (and many men too) find such material distasteful. We suspect that there are more customers who abhor these magazines than there are those who enjoy them. We hope that when they discover the strength of public opinion, newsagents will reconsider their decisions to stock such magazines.

Christian Action is a group of Christians from various churches in the Congleton area who unite to act on moral and ethical matters. If anyone would like to know more about the group they should telephone Congleton 234.

ENDS

Example: a press release.

- Typing. Your press release stands a much better chance of being read if it is typed. Leave approximately 4cm space either side of the typing, and use double spacing so that journalists can alter the text. Try to avoid underlining words, as this is a signal to the typesetter to use italics, which is a matter for the editor to consider.
- Photographs. Always try to provide a 'picture angle' if you can: stories accompanied by a photograph stand out better and often have a bigger headline. A picture helps to present your campaign in a straight-forward manner.

If you have a particularly important story to release, consider holding a press conference where reporters will have the chance to question your spokesman on the details of the story. However, you should only use this method of releasing your story if it really is important: local papers do not have the time or the staff to devote to anything other than major conferences. Usually you will get a better response through written press releases and personal or telephone contact.

Letters to the editor

Your first attempts at letter writing will probably be to official bodies, such as the council, when you are making your initial protest or attempt to persuade the officials to your point of view. When you approach councillors for support, and when you submit formal objections to planning applications, or when you send in the results of reports and surveys, you will have to write concise, clear letters, setting out your point of view or summarising the contents of your longer documents. (See following page.)

But letter-writing can also be used in another way: to generate support and free publicity for your cause. Most regional and local newspapers have a letters page or correspondence column where letters from readers to the editor are printed. These are often the most widely read sections of

10 Church Lane
Barton
Midchester

Mr J. Smith
Parks and Recreation Department
Town Hall
Midchester

Dear Mr Smith,
    I understand from our telephone conversation today that the council is considering terminating the free swimming facilities it offers to over-60s.
    I wish to register a strong protest at such a move. To deny these facilities to a section of the population who have little opportunity to use most of our available leisure amenities is unfair. Few Senior Citizens wish to use the tennis courts or the roller skating rink or the BMX track; for many of them swimming is a healthy and a sociable pastime which should be encouraged. Many of them are unwilling to go out in the evening, and the daytime free swim is an opportunity to meet their friends. I should also point out that although their swim is free, they often stay for a cup of tea in the pool cafe afterwards, adding to the revenue there.
    I urge the council not to withdraw this valuable concession.
        Yours sincerely,

Example: a letter of protest.

the newspaper, and can provide one of the best media for getting your message across.

Letters can be used to comment on something that has already been written in the paper or magazine, or that has recently taken place; to reply to points from other letter-writers, or from opponents; to raise new issues or start a debate on a topical subject; to support a campaign which the local group is already organising; to thank people for supporting a campaign or event.

Letters should be short: if they are too long the editor is likely to cut them or leave them out altogether. Decide what point you wish to make, and keep to it. Type your letter if at all possible, and remember to include your name and address (most papers will not publish the letter otherwise, and they may wish to check on its authenticity).

Anyone can write a letter. Individual letters can make a point effectively, but much more impact can be made if a whole series of letters can be arranged. To organise this, you should consider setting up a letter-writing panel.

A letter-writing panel consists of a group of people who are willing either to write letters to the newspapers themselves, or to allow their signatures to be used on letters drafted by the panel organiser. There is nothing underhand in this — a quick glance at the correspondence columns will often provide evidence that other groups already have their own panels operating.

Panel members raise issues and then support each other's points of view — the aim is to give the impression that there is a whole body of public opinion in the area, agreeing on a particular point. Published letters can make an issue gain importance, and a series of letters can give added credibility to a local campaign.

A panel is easily organised. Members are usually ordinary group members who don't mind their names appearing in print occasionally, but they may include friends or other members of your church. Try to use people who are not widely known to be members of your core group: letters from 'ordinary' members of the public supporting your viewpoint will be more convincing than letters from the group chairman supporting himself!

Each week you should arrange for two or three letters to be sent to the newspapers concerned. They may support each other, expand points made in the previous week's paper, or comment on a particular issue, but they should not be almost identical in style or content. Some panel members may be willing to write their own letters, though they may appreciate advice on what to write. Others will prefer you to draft their letters for them, so that all they have to do is type or write it in their own hand, sign it, and post it.

If you have members with journalistic experience, or who are used to writing advertising copy, seek their help in drafting letters — they can ensure that you write hard-hitting, point-scoring letters that are much more likely to be published.

Make your letters interesting and brief; be accurate and justify the views you put forward. Replies from the opposition should encourage you — it means that you are worrying them, and provides you with an opportunity to respond. Never get involved in sarcastic or petty point-scoring: a factual, well-argued letter will create a better impression. If possible, try to be in the driving seat, forcing the opposition to reply to your points, rather than being on the defensive yourself.

A successful letter-writing panel will generate other supporting letters from readers unconnected with your group. For instance, if your writers start voicing concern about council plans to grant a licence to a sex shop, other people are likely to write and support your view. Your original writers can then respond by suggesting a local public meeting on the subject, and the core group can then enter the fray officially by organising the meeting themselves. This will generate further publicity in the news columns, while you organise further letters praising the group for staging the meeting! (See following page.)

Remember, letters which begin 'Dear Mr —' end 'Yours sincerely', and those which begin 'Dear Sir' end with 'Yours faithfully'.

10 Church Lane
Barton
Midchester

The Editor
Midchester Gazette
Midchester

Dear Sir,

Following the correspondence in your columns about the proposed closure of the Barton village school, I last night attended a public meeting held in the school hall by the Barton Christian Action Group. Mr Bloggs, the County Chief Education Officer, was present to answer questions from parents and local residents.

One of the main points made was that the school offers not just an education for the children but also a meeting place and focus for village life.

I should like to congratulate the Barton Christian Action Group for enabling this lively public debate to take place. It is good to see that there are still people who care about the life of our community.

Yours faithfully,

Example: a letter to the press.

Clearly, a letter-writing panel will have the most impact if it is well organised and the majority of members are not well-known CARE supporters. Always be on the lookout for new members, and do not use the same names every week.

The panel organiser should keep a 'cuttings file' of all letters published, and of any responses from opposition or supporters. This is important as you may want to quote from a previous letter several months later, or point out the contradictions in letters from your opponents. You should also keep a copy of every letter which you send. A good filing system is an essential tool to ensure that your panel is as effective as possible.

Following a report on BBC2's *Newsnight*, when the wide availability of child pornography and the means for contact for paedophiles was uncovered, Portsmouth Area Family Concern initiated a correspondence with the publishers of *Exchange and Mart*, the newspaper mentioned in the programme. The group provided United Newspapers with information and further evidence of the way in which paedophiles used the advertisements, and told the company that their style of advertising provided paedophiles with excuses for their behaviour and contacts which enabled them to obtain hard core and child pornography. The publishers decided to reject call lines, together with adult films, books and magazines from the Adult Interest category. A House of Commons motion tabled by six MPs 'recognised the part played by the Portsmouth Area Family Concern in achieving this policy decision'.

Press files

A good campaigner or press officer will keep a 'cuttings file' of relevant items from the regional and local newspapers. You should keep cuttings referring to your own activities and those of your opponents, and should file them so that you can locate any item easily. A good method is to use a box file and divide it into sections with cardboard folders — you may want sections for your MP (any speeches, photographs or activities in which your MP is mentioned); core group (reports of campaigns, activities, etc); letters (from the local newspapers, both your letters and those of the opposition, and any others of interest); and general (including items of local interest, and also regional and national material which may be useful).

You should keep a separate box file of all your press releases, together with a record of how many of your releases are published, and how your press coverage compares with that of other groups (measure it in single column inches — how much space is devoted to your activities, and how much to your opponents?).

Stick each cutting on a sheet of A4 paper with Pritt or Cow Gum, and write next to it the name of the newspaper and the date when it appeared. Use one side of the paper only, for easy reference.

Whoever takes on the task of filing material needs to obtain copies of all the local papers (including the free ones), and to keep the files up to date — a retired person with time to do the job properly may be the best choice.

Media monitor

Linked with the task of handling the press files is the work of your media monitor. Obviously most members of your group will want to keep abreast of current events and topical issues, but few campaigners will be able to read every paper or watch and listen to every news bulletin. So it may be worth appointing a group member who is at home most of the time to monitor the media. If this person is already handling the press files, the local papers will already be covered, but a good monitor should also listen to the local radio and television news at least once or twice a day, and keep a note of reports which may require a reaction from your group.

Media monitors usually keep the rest of the group informed about any press reports which they may have missed, and contact the press officer about anything which may need an immediate response. In addition, they listen to the views expressed in radio 'phone-in' programmes, and either phone in a comment themselves or contact someone else who is able to do so. They also keep a watch for signs of bias, such as radio debates which make assumptions which are contrary to the Christian view. Complaints should be made to the relevant authority in such cases.

During election campaigns it is important that someone listens in to what each of the candidates has to say on family issues — particularly with reference to life issues and obscenity. Quick responses and questions put to candidates can reinforce their awareness of these matters as vote-catchers.

Being interviewed

Being interviewed by the media may seem a daunting prospect, but you should generally take advantage of the opportunity. After all, practice makes perfect! Here are some key rules for you to follow when preparing:

- Agree the scope of the interview
- Remember that the interview is not a battle, with a 'winner' at the end
- Find out if any other people are taking part in the feature
- Decide the main points you want to get across
- Accept the constraints of time, but realise that a great deal can be said in two or three minutes
- The advantage of radio is that you can hold a note in your hand as a reminder of the main points you wish to cover
- Anticipate difficult questions
- Remember that the interviewer will ask the questions that the listener wants to ask
- Keep your answers short
- Identify your audience
- Recognise the possibility of another point of view

- A sense of humour comes over well, but so does insincerity
- Feel free to talk in a conversational way

Radio phone-ins

National and local radio phone-in programmes are a useful way of contributing to public debate about contemporary issues, but do remember the following:

- Do not read out a question or general contribution, as it will always sound stilted
- Keep your question short
- Don't cram more than one or two points into each contribution
- Be ready with a supplementary point/question
- Be courteous
- Don't be frightened to say that something is untrue, if that is the case
- If the lines are busy, keep trying
- Make sure your radio is turned down when you are due to go on air

Television

You will not often be called upon to present your case on television, but do take the opportunity if it is offered. Television is the major mass communication medium today, and a TV interview is likely to reach far more people than a local newspaper article or radio report.

Communicating effectively on television is a skill, and some practice is invaluable: it may be worth funding one member to go on a training course if one is available in your area. However, do not let lack of experience prevent you from accepting an invitation to appear on television.

You are most likely to be invited to join a studio audience for a discussion programme like 'Question Time', especially if your group has written to the broadcasting station asking to be considered for audience invitations. When you arrive in the studio, try to find a seat where the cameras are likely to notice you: the front row is better than the back. If you get a chance to speak, keep your contribution brief and to the point. When called, wait for a second or two before starting to speak, to allow the studio microphone and the cameras to focus on you. Speak normally, clearly, and not too fast, but don't ramble or the presenter is likely to stop you in mid-sentence.

Even when you have finished your question, don't assume the camera has left you. It may continue to show your reactions to whatever reply is made to your contribution, and the microphone may pick up any muttered comment you make. Remain alert throughout the programme, look interested in case the camera captures your face for a moment, but keep your own eyes on the 'stage' — don't keep trying to ascertain which camera is being used at any particular moment.

If you are invited to do an interview on any campaign or issue, make sure you know your facts before the interview begins. Keep calm throughout — don't let the camera capture a look of horror or frustration. Decide in advance which points you wish to make, and make them irrespective of what questions you are asked. Smile and look either at the interviewer or at the camera. Don't look down at the ground, and don't let mannerisms creep in (such as scratching your head or rubbing your hands together).

Ensure that television stations, like radio and newspaper reporters, know who to contact for your group's viewpoint at any time: communication has to be two-way!

Media Awareness Project

If you would like to develop your basic media presentational skills and understanding of how the media works, get in touch with the Media Awareness Project. They run training courses around the country, and are funded by one of the Sainsbury family charitable trusts. They are at 24 Tufton Street, London SW1P 3RB (tel 071–222 5533).

5 Extra Know-how

Public meetings

Holding a public meeting is one of the most basic ways of getting or measuring support on an issue. However, like all the methods discussed here, they have to be good to be successful. Badly organised or poorly thought-out meetings are just as likely to lose you support and goodwill.

The first step is to assess why you want a meeting, who you want to come, and what you would like the outcome to be. You may wish to find out what matters are generally felt to be important; to discuss and plan some action; to explain your views on an issue, perhaps as a way of starting or maintaining a campaign; to listen to or to confront experts or councillors; to form a core group; to generate publicity; or to keep a group open and democratic by holding an Annual General Meeting.

Planning

Public meetings usually consist of four parts. The start consists of prayer, a welcoming statement, a short explanation of the reason for the meeting, and a brief outline of how you want the meeting to run. The middle consists of speeches or statements from the core group of organisers, speeches by others (such as members, councillors or experts, and comments from the audience. The finish consists of suggestions and resolutions on action, a summarising statement, any appeals for donations, membership or help, and details of future meetings; it is followed by the socialising time, when people mingle and chat after the meeting has formally closed.

Try to keep meetings fairly short: about one and a half hours is ideal. After two hours you will find that you are losing your audience's attention, and people will leave.

A day or so before the meeting get the organisers together for a 'pre-meeting meeting', to check that all the arrangements have been made; all the various tasks should already have been allocated so that all your members know what they are supposed to be doing.

Perhaps the most important job is that of the chairman; he should open the meeting and explain what it is about, and introduce each speaker. He must keep the meeting in order and make sure that only one person speaks at a time; but also make sure that everyone who wishes gets an opportunity to speak. He must prevent speakers from going on for too long (so he should keep an eye on the time) and he should be sensitive to the feeling of the meeting and watch for signs of boredom. He must keep people to the agenda, and direct questions to the people who can or should answer them. Finally, he must summarise and end the meeting.

However, there are many other tasks which members have to undertake to ensure the smooth running of your meeting.

- If you are inviting outside speakers — such as councillors or experts — make sure someone is responsible for all contact with them. Give them plenty of notice and provide them with a broad idea of what is going to be discussed, and also a time limit (or else they may dominate the meeting). Make sure they know the location — send them a map if necessary.
- Stewards show people to their seats and may have to keep

order if necessary; this makes people feel welcome to the meeting and reassures them that it has been organised.

- A secretary should keep a record of what happens, although this does not have to be as complete a record as the minutes of a routine meeting.
- Refreshments are especially useful as an informal way of approaching people, if you want them to get involved in your group: providing a cup of tea or coffee after the meeting makes a good reason to stay and chat.
- It is useful to have a record of who came to the meeting, so make one person responsible for an attendance list, and ask everyone to write down their names and addresses, probably as they arrive, so that you can contact them again.
- A literature stall offers useful publicity — any books, leaflets or newsletters people take away with them may help to generate support for your cause. A stall is also another opening for interested individuals to get into conversation and ask questions about your group.
- If you want to make a cash collection you should put stewards with collecting boxes near the exits — don't pass a plate along the rows!
- If you decide to enliven your meeting with a film or video, rather than using a whole series of speakers, make sure that someone is responsible for obtaining not just the film but also any screens or projection equipment you may need. Check out the availability of black-out facilities and the type of plugs and cables you need well in advance. If you are using a television set make sure it is large enough for everyone to see. Check also on the copyright of the film or video: you may need a licence to show it to a public audience.
- Check that your publicity is effective and in the right places: it's no good organising a meeting that no one knows about. Have you put up posters, advertised in the press, and told people what is happening?

During the April 1992 general election campaign, Christians came together in hundreds of local areas to interview parliamentary candidates as part of the Christian Election Forum. One sitting MP remarked that it was the best public meeting he had ever attended.

Throughout the planning stages you should bear in mind the purpose of the meeting: if you want to take a particular action, you should have thought out a motion beforehand so that people can vote on it at the meeting. A good motion should identify the motion's sponsors, explain why the motion is needed, and state the right attitude or opinion. If it is calling for action it must also say who should take action and what action should be taken.

Motions need to be proposed and seconded before they can be voted on by the meeting: make sure that a couple of members take on the responsibility to do this at the meeting. After a motion has been voted on and agreed it is then called a resolution.

When members at the meeting want to alter the wording and meaning of a motion, the wording or change they put forward is called an amendment. This must specify whether words are to be added or deleted, say where the change should be, and give the exact wording of the change.

Use the following checklist for running the meeting itself.

- Get there early — people may turn up well before time and you need to make sure everything is in order (someone is bound to forget something!)
- Arrange the seats to create either a formal or an informal atmosphere, as you choose. Keep the audience and the speakers as close together as possible.
- Just before the start, make sure a few of the core group

meet to pray and ask God's blessing on the meeting. A small group may want to pray throughout the meeting, too!

- Make sure people are welcomed and guest speakers recognised.
- Put a jug of water and glasses on the table for the speakers.
- If the meeting is particularly large, make sure there are plenty of stewards, and that they are briefed about what to do in the event of a fire, particularly for those in wheelchairs.
- Make sure all stewards know where the toilets are situated. Start on time — it makes a good impression.
- Try to keep contributions short and to the point.
- Make sure the meeting is clear about what action has been decided on and what people can do to help.
- Try to finish early, especially if the informal meeting of people afterwards is felt to be important.
- Tidy up and thank the caretaker, especially if you wish to use the room again!

Remember that it is important to look back after any activity and see what can be learned — either about new aspects of the issue which have emerged, or simply about your own organisation and skills. You should write a press release as soon as possible, before the public forgets about the meeting. If people have volunteered to help with any task, get them to work quickly before their enthusiasm fades.

Making speeches

Most people get nervous about speaking in public, so it helps if the burden is shared by a group: when you are setting out your case get one person to give the background, another the solutions, a third the action you want to take, and so on. Even so, you may have difficulty in persuading your members that they can stand up and make a speech! There are, however, a few simple rules which help to overcome many of the problems.

First, prayer. Any Christian speaker must prepare through prayer, even when making the preliminary plans. Spend a few minutes in thoughtful prayer before you put pen to paper, and read any relevant passages of scripture.

Expect to be nervous. All good speakers are nervous before they begin, however well they manage to conceal it. The best solution is to be well prepared, know what you want to say and do some rehearsing — and timing — in private.

Be yourself. Try to be as natural as possible, using your normal everyday language, accent and pronunciation. Don't try to sound like a newsreader or like any well-known speaker you have heard. Your job is to get your message across: audiences respond to enthusiasm and a belief in what you are saying. You are likely to lose these qualities if you start aping professional speakers.

Know your subject. Make sure everything you say is based on fact, and use plenty of practical examples of what you mean. Don't use any facts or statistics you don't fully understand.

Know your audience. Ask yourself how much the audience already knows about the subject, why they have come to the meeting, and what they expect to hear. The answers to these questions should influence what you say and how you say it. Thus, if your audience knows very little about the subject, you should avoid technical jargon.

Know what you want to achieve. Are you trying to convey information, explain a course of action, or get people's support? For instance, if you are trying to get a discussion started, you should try to ask questions rather than make statements.

Decide what to say. Start by jotting down the main points you wish to include, and then be ruthless! Get rid of anything which is not strictly relevant, and put the remaining points in a sensible order. Many speakers claim that they say everything three times: 'Tell them what you're going to say, tell them, then tell them what you've just told them' — but not in the same words every time, of course!

Speeches need a beginning, a middle and an end. You should start by introducing yourself and the subject, perhaps with a story or an example. Laughter is a useful way of relaxing the audience and getting attention, but avoid anything too dramatic. Once you have made the subject clear, you should give the full message. Give concrete examples, explain your reasons and make clear your advice and suggestions. Try to make your points logically and leave your most telling or important point to the end. Finish by giving a brief summary and state how the audience can help with the problems. Thank people for listening and the organisers for their work.

Make sure you don't talk for too long. People may lose interest if they have to listen to one voice for more than about twenty minutes. Ten to fifteen minutes is even better, where possible. Avoid sidetracks or rambling stories.

Prepare for questions. Work out answers beforehand to the most obvious questions, and if you don't know the answer, say so.

Use notes. If you write out your speech in full and read it, your delivery will be dull and you will be unable to look at the audience. On the other hand, trying to speak 'off the cuff' is fraught with danger — you may forget some points altogether. The best solution is to write out the main headings of your speech on postcards — use large, clear writing and use one side of the card only. Number the cards in case they get dropped!

Don't speak too fast. Nervousness is likely to make you want to hurry, but you must speak clearly to be heard. You sound much more interesting, too, if you vary your pace, and are not afraid to pause. Silence can be very effective.

Use feedback. If you are interrupted by your audience, you can try to ignore them — though this may be difficult if people are shouting. It is better to promise to deal with the point later, or ask them to wait until question time. At least you are getting a response! Many speakers (like comedians) have a collection of suitable replies to interruptions. Another form of feedback is people's expressions: they may look puzzled, bored, or fidget. You can use this as a signal to explain a point more carefully, vary your delivery, or use a visual aid.

Make your ending clear. Try to end on a high note — don't let your speech fade away. The easiest way to do this is to restate the most important points.

Review your performance. Get friends to comment on your speech so you can improve for next time.

Reports

A report on its own will do very little: it must be seen as part of your general campaign tactics. It can be a useful way of starting a campaign, or as a basis for lobbying, providing the details to back up your arguments. Because of this, you need to give careful thought to what you include in the report — you may want to keep back some arguments for later use.

Reports can be very useful in helping you to assess your arguments: the work involved in producing a good report forces you to work out your position carefully. They may also gain you some publicity, and enable you to make a full statement of your argument. If your report is good and detailed, it will gain you respect: people will listen to what you say. It will also make your opponents think again about their actions and proposals: detailed reports need detailed answers.

However, there are some negative aspects which you should consider before starting to write a report. Firstly, reports take time and money to produce. They may slow you up at a time when you need to act quickly, and use up precious financial reserves. Secondly, your opponents may have the resources to 'out-report' or 'out-statistic' you. The debate may become tied up in figures and details rather than concentrating on the principles. Thirdly, your report has to be good. If the arguments are easily broken down because you have not done your homework, your cause may lose support. There is always the chance, too, that a report gives away too much of your thinking; in a campaign where one of your major weapons is surprise, you may give the opposition time to prepare their replies. Fourthly, don't try to be too comprehensive. If weak arguments are mixed with strong ones, your opponents will try to ensure that the strong are ignored and the deficiencies in the weak arguments are pointed out.

So you should think very hard before tying up effort in producing reports — perhaps a fact sheet would be a more effective way of using the information you have.

Next, you must know who the report is aimed at, as this will affect how you write it and what sort of details you include. Usually it is aimed at the decision-makers — MPs, councillors, officials, etc, but different groups have different viewpoints. Anyone who relies on election — such as an MP or a local councillor — will be interested in the political effect of an issue, public opinion and vote-catching. Officials may be more impressed with detailed arguments, facts and figures. Technical experts will want to see the scientific arguments. Make sure you have a target audience when you begin.

Format

You should include only accurate facts and figures: leave out anything you are not sure of. But you may include arguments and opinions — whether your own or other people's — and your recommended solutions to the problem. Back up your arguments with photographs, plans and drawings if they help. There is a generally accepted format for reports, and you should follow the outline below.

● Summary and conclusions. The main points should be set out briefly at the beginning so that the report is easier to understand. Keep this section brief and to the point but try to cover all the important issues.

- Introduction. This should set the scene, and explain why your group is interested and what the problem is. It may be useful to say what the problem is not.

- History and background. The background is usually provided in date order — explaining what matters developed first and what has happened up to the present. Quote from any documents (eg council minutes, letters and replies, press cuttings, other reports) and always state the source, date and author of any quotes.

- The problem as you see it. Make this statement as clear as possible, using any evidence you have gathered from reports, surveys, interviewing people and so on.

- Discussion. You may want to expand on your findings, comparing them with other people's views. Don't be afraid to summarise the main points again at the end.

- Appendices. If you need an appendix it may include details of how you did your survey, or evidence provided by other groups.

When you are writing your report there are several points to bear in mind. You should always remember your target audience, and consider how you are going to keep their attention. Even the cover may help you — an interesting front page encourages the reader. Try to keep the whole report fairly short, as long reports rarely get read in full, especially in busy council offices or by MPs deluged with paperwork. Remember to put a summary and a list of recommendations at the beginning; that may be the only part that is read!

Avoid jargon and long words; they will not make your work look any more 'professional'. The aim is to write something that is easy to read and easily understood. For the same reason you should vary the presentation, using pictures, maps, tables and diagrams — even cartoons — to hold the

Hemel Hempstead Christian Concern

Telephone:
1234 54321
                                        21 Blank Road
                                        Hemel Hempstead

Licensing Officer
Local Licences Dept
County Hall
Hertford SG13 8DJ

Dear Sir,

Re: Sex Shop Licence Application, 193 London Road,
Apsley

Please find attached the formal objection, prepared by Hemel Hempstead Christian Concern, to the licence application by Darker Enterprises Ltd. Our objection includes the following:

1. Document entitled 'Sex Shop licensing — a Discussion of our Responsibilities'
2. Survey of Apsley Community Centre relating to regular usage of the premises, especially for activities of minors.
3. Statistics relating to the number of pedestrian visitors to the junction of London Road, Storey Street and Durrants Hill.
4. Petition in excess of 640 names collected across Dacorum, but centred especially around the Apsley community.

You will note that the objection in all cases seeks to establish that (a) the sex shop is highly unsuited to its position close to shops, church and community centre, and (b) any such establishment is unwanted by the residents throughout the area. We believe that the council should state that 'nil' is the appropriate number of sex shops in Dacorum.

I trust that the enclosed will be given careful considera- tion, bearing in mind the broad level of support shown.

Yours faithfully,
on behalf of Hemel Hempstead Christian Concern

Example: a letter accompanying a formal objection.

reader's interest. A clear layout also helps: break up the material into well-labelled sections, perhaps using different coloured paper for different sections, and consider numbering the paragraphs. All these techniques make it easier for people to find things when discussing the report.

Remember to end your report where you began — with the conclusions. Finally, get someone else to check it for sense, spelling, grammar and typographical errors.

Use

On national issues reports are often produced centrally by CARE, using the evidence submitted to a Government committee by interested parties. Local groups usually pro- duce reports on local issues, such as a proposed new sex shop or the planned opening of an abortion clinic.

No matter how good your report writing is, it will not help your campaign if the report fails to reach the right people at the right time. You need to send your report to the people who matter — that is, the people you are trying to influence, the press, and your members. Each may need a different approach.

When giving the report to the media, you should not just send a copy to the newspapers and local radio and television stations. Visit them in person and take the reporters through the report, explaining any important issues. Get your timing right, so that you know when the press deadlines are: try to have news items appearing at the same time as the decision-makers receive the report, so that they will pay more attention to it.

When presenting your report to the decision-makers you may not be able to see them in person right away, so include a covering letter saying why they should read and support the report. Always try to follow it up quickly with a personal visit and some energetic lobbying, so the MP, councillors, etc., will realise that you represent a large body of opinion.

If the report is long some of your members and the general public may not ever read it thoroughly; consider producing a fact sheet, covering the main points of the case, for distribution to the community. You can always refer to the report so that people who are really interested can follow it up.

Finally, remember that although a report may involve a great deal of effort, it is only part of your campaign. Use it alongside other techniques, and don't allow all your other activities to grind to a halt while you are working on it.

Printing

When you are putting your message across on paper, whether through words or pictures, you will need to produce some printed material. Some groups use a professional printing firm, while others use their own printing equipment.

The most useful equipment to have access to is a word processor: with the boom in such technology any group is likely to know someone who will be willing to produce newsletters or other documents for them. The more sophisticated word processors, with desktop publishing packages, can produce very professional results indeed. But if you cannot beg or borrow access to such a machine, don't worry. Use a good-quality typewriter and some Letraset letters for headings, and make a friend of your local printing firm.

Text

If, instead of typing, you decide to use a typesetting firm, check that the type will be set in the style and size you prefer (give clear instructions). When the typesetting is delivered, check it carefully for errors in the text. There is a difference in the way type is measured for a typewriter and for typesetting: on a typewriter, the larger the number, the smaller the type size (typewriter points = characters per inch); in typesetting, the larger the number, the larger the type size — don't confuse the two! Most typewriters use 12-point type, but modern electronic typewriters may offer 10-point and 15-point as well. In typesetting, 10- or 11-point is the usual size, while headings and sub-headings may use 24-point or 18-point.

Headings

Headings are often produced from Letraset or other dry transfer lettering. Many art and design shops stock a wide range of styles and sizes, and if you are producing your own headings and artwork, you will need to collect a small stock yourself. Ask for a catalogue from your local stockist, and choose those you like (Helvetica Bold, Gill Sans, Univers, Folio and Futura are popular; for the more adventurous, there are Flash, Roundel or Fumo Dropshadow). Letraset can be used from 24-point to 48-point for headings and titles, and 16-point to 24-point for sub-headings.

Style

Borders and illustrations should be used to break up the monotony of black print. A good cartoon can be used to emphasise a particular point, and may do so better than a thousand words. If your cartoon or artwork is too big for the space available, it can easily be reduced in size on a modern photocopier. Your local instant print shop should be able to do the work while you wait, for only a few pence per sheet.

If you wish to include photographs in your artwork, ensure

the original print is clear and sharp. It should be black and white, preferably taken by a professional photographer or at least by an amateur with a good camera . If you are printing by offset litho, the photographs need to be screened — broken down into thousands of tiny dots. Check with the printer what screen is best, as they are measured by the number of dots to the square inch.

For added impact you can use a 'reverse block' — white lettering on a black background. You can use a sheet of black paper cut to size, or a piece of white paper carefully shaded with black felt tip (not ballpoint). This can be used to good effect on posters and window bills as well as newsletters.

Printing is normally done in black ink on white paper, as this is cheapest and easiest to read. However, the use of coloured paper can be dramatic, and so can the use of more than one colour of ink — though this can be expensive, so consider whether the extra cost is worth while.

Posters

Visual publicity is an important element in any campaign, and a good poster helps to keep your issue in the public eye: it may be seen by thousands of people every day.

First, get an attractive design and make your poster stand out: it should be clear and colourful, and get your message across. Remember that people may only catch a glimpse of it as they pass, so don't use too many words. A simple slogan works well, particularly on larger posters or prominent sites. If your campaign has a logo — a simple design which appears on all literature — use it in the posters too: the more times people see it, the more likely they are to remember it.

Having decided on the design and the size of the print run, plan your poster campaign. You may concentrate on getting posters on the main roads first, with appropriate permission from the local council, or in the windows of your supporters, or on church notice boards. Consider how to ensure that the posters are actually displayed after you have distributed them — a poster which already has gum arabic, double-sided tape or Blu-tac on it stands a better chance of being put up than one without. Better still, try to stick the poster up yourself before leaving the church or shop.

Don't be over-ambitious: decide what visual publicity you can afford and have the manpower to make and erect — it's no good having a thousand posters printed and then only managing to get fifty of them stuck up in shop windows. Appoint a co-ordinating officer for your poster campaign who will distribute and check up on posters.

Finally, don't forget the imprint on all your printed material. You should include the publisher's and printer's name and address at the foot of all leaflets and on the face of all posters. If your produce a leaflet which is designed to be stuck up as a poster or window bill, the imprint must appear on the face of the part intended for display.

SECTION 4

RESOURCES

1 Further Reading

The case for action

Alison, M. and Edwards, D. (eds) *Christianity and Conservatism*. Hodder & Stoughton, 1990.

Alton, D. *Faith in Britain*. Hodder & Stoughton, 1991.

Andrews, D. *Can You Hear the Heartbeat? A Challenge to Care the Way Jesus Cared*. Hodder Christian paperbacks, 1989.

Beckett, F. *Called to Action*. Fount Paperbacks, 1989.

Bloesch, D. *Crumbling Foundations*. Zondervan, 1984.

Cameron, N. *The Logic of Christian Political Responsibility*. CARE Booklet no 2.

Colson, C. *Against the Night*. Word Books.

Colson, C. *The God of Stones and Spiders*. Hodder & Stoughton.

Henry, C. *Aspects of Christian Social Ethics*. Baker, 1980.

Henry, C. *Twilight of a Great Civilization: The Drift Towards Neopaganism*. Crossway Books, USA, 1990.

Holmes, A. *Ethics*. IVP, 1984.

Kantzer, K. S. et al. *The Christian as Citizen*. CTI, 1985.

Lamb, C. *Belief in a Mixed Society*. Lion, 1985.

Lewis, C. S. *The Abolition of Man*. Collins/Fount. 1978.

Marshall, P. *Thine is the Kingdom*. Marshall, Morgan & Scott, 1984.

McCloughry, R. *Taking Action*. Frameworks, 1990.

Miller, P. *Into the Arena*. Kingsway, 1992.
Newbigin, L. *Foolishness to the Greeks*. SPCK, 1986.
Newbigin, L. *Truth to Tell: The Gospel as Public Truth*, SPCK.
Schaeffer, F. *A Christian Manifesto*. Crossway Books, 1981.
Stott, J. *Issues Facing Christians Today*. Marshalls, 1984.
Williams, S. *The Kingdom of God*. CARE Booklet no. 9.
Wright, C. *Human Rights: A Study in Biblical Themes*. Grove Books, 1979.

Biography

Holman, R. *Good Old George: The Life of George Lansbury*. Lion.
Lean, G. *God's Politician: William Wilberforce's Struggle*. Darton, Longman & Todd, 1980.
Pollock, J. *Wilberforce*. Lion, 1986.
Pollock, J. *Shaftesbury: The Poor Man's Earl*. Hodder & Stoughton, 1985.

Education

Considering Christian Schools. CiE.
Cooling, Trevor and Oliver, George. *Church and School*. Grove Books, UK, 1989.
Cooling, Margaret. *Assemblies for Primary Schools: Autumn Term*. Wheaton, UK, 1990.
Cooling, Margaret. *Assemblies for Primary Schools: Spring Term*. Wheaton, UK, 1990.
Cooling, Trevor, and Roques, Mark. *Christian Student Teachers' Book List*. CiE.
Cunnington, Howard. *Your Turn to Take Assembly*. Association of Christian Teachers, UK, 1989.
Deakin, Ruth. *Report on the New Independent Christian Schools*. CiE.

Guidelines for Group Discussion on Education. CiE.

Halloween – an information paper. CiE.

Holt, Anne. *Being a School Governor.* CiE.

King, Janet. *Leading Worship in Schools.* Monarch, UK, 1990.

King, Janet. *52 Ideas for Secondary Classroom Assemblies.* Monarch, 1992.

Martin, Charles. *Schools Now.* Lion, UK, 1989.

Multi-cultural Education – Some Points for Christian Parents. CiE.

Oliver, George. *Praying About Education – Especially Schools.* CiE.

Oliver, George. *Suggestions towards a Christian Programme of Religious Education for Primary Schools.* CiE.

Oliver, George. *Handling Our Christian Commitment in the Classroom, or, Ten Tips for Tightrope Walkers!* CiE.

Owen, Roger. *Parent's Guide 5–11.* Kingsway, UK, 1988.

Planning an Education Meeting. An advisory paper. CiE.

Roques, Mark. *Curriculum Unmasked.* Monarch, UK, 1989.

School Support Service File. CiE.

Sex Education Policy Document. CARE.

Towards a New Sexual Revolution: Guidelines for governors and parents. Joint publication by CARE, CiE, OCU. UK, 1988.

Williams, Tricia. *Christians in School?* Scripture Union, 1985.

Issues

AIDS Care. The Salvation Army, 1988.

Atkinson, D. *Life and Death.* OUP, 1986.

Billingsley, K. *The Seductive Image: A Christian Critique of the World of Film.* Crossway Books, 1989.

Blue, R. *The Debt Squeeze: How Your Family Can Become Financially Free.* Focus on the Family, 1989.

Bowers, F. *Who's This Sitting in My Pew? Mentally Handicapped People in the Church.* Triangle, 1988.

Bowers, F. (ed.) *Let Love be Genuine: Mental Handicap and the Church*. Baptist Union, 1985.

Cameron, N. *The Kindness That Kills*. CARE Booklet no 1.

Cameron, N. and Sims, P. *Abortion: The Crisis in Morals and Medicine*. IVP, 1986.

CARE. Picking up the Pieces: an action pack on pornography.

Chandler, R. *Understanding the New Age*. Word Books.

Christian Awareness Pack on Mental Handicap. Joint publication by CARE, A cause for Concern, Christian Impact & Scripture Union.

Coffey, I. *No Stranger in the City*. IVP.

Collier, Caroline. *The Twentieth Century Plague*. Lion Publishing, 1990.

Collins, Gary. *Christian Counselling*. Word Books, 1989.

Comiskey, Andrew. *Pursuing Sexual Wholeness*. Monarch, 1990.

David, Alison. *From Where I Sit*. Triangle, 1989.

Dixon, P. *The Truth About AIDS*. Kingsway, 1990.

Elkington, J. and Hailes, J. *The Green Consumer Guide*. Gollancz, 1988.

Elliot, C. *Signs of Our Times: Prayer and Action to Change the World*. Marshalls, 1988.

George, B. *The Almond Tree: Pastoral care of Mentally Handicapped People*. Collins, 1987.

Hallett, Martin. *I Am Learning to Love*. Marshall, Morgan & Scott, 1989.

Hancock, Maxine. *Child Sexual Abuse*. Harold Shaw Publishers, USA, 1990.

Hill, Debbie. *Timothy – Mission Accomplished*. New Wine Press, 1990.

Huggett, J. *Life in a Sex-Mad Society*. Frameworks, 1990.

Jenkins, G. *Cohabitation: A Biblical Perspective*. Grove Ethical Studies no 84, Grove Books, 1992.

Keay, K. *How to Make the World Less Hungry*. Frameworks, 1990.

Kohner, N. *Caring at Home*. Health Education Authority and King's Fund.

Ledger, C. *Caring for the Carers*. Kingsway, 1992.

Lessons in Love: Seven Talks to Teens on Sex and Relationships. CARE Videos, 1990.

Living Dangerously: Euthanasia Examined. CARE Videos 1992.

Logan, K. *Paganism and the Occult*. Kingsway, 1988.

Logan, P. *A Life to be Lived: Homelessness and Pastoral Care*. DLT, 1989.

Makower, F. *Faith or Folly? Drugs, Ministry and Community*. Darton, Longman & Todd, 1989.

Marriage Matters (Parts 1 and 2). CARE Videos, 1991.

McCloughry and Bebawi. *AIDS: A Christian Response*. Grove Books, 1989.

McDowell, J. *How to Help Your Child Say 'No' to Sexual Pressure*. Word Books, 1988.

Moate, M. and Enoch, D. *Schizophrenia: Voices in the Dark*. Kingsway, 1990.

Moberly, E. *Homosexuality: A New Christian Ethic*, James Clarke, 1983.

Morgan, H. *Through Peter's Eyes*. Arthur James, 1990.

Payne, Leanne. *Real Presence: The Christian World View of C.S. Lewis*. Monarch, 1989.

Pollard, B. *Euthanasia: Should We Kill the Dying?* Mount.

Porter, D. *User's Guide to the Media*. IVP, 1988.

Potter, D. *Too Soon to Die*. Evangelical Press.

Potter, D. and Potter, M. *We're All Special to God*. Scripture Union, 1990.

Robertson, Jenny. *Abuse Within the Family*. Creative Publishing, 1987.

Schaeffer, F. and Koop, C. E. *Whatever Happened to the Human Race?* Marshall, Morgan & Scott, 1980.

Smith, A. *The Euthanasia Debate: The Living Alternative*. St Francis Hospice.

Spring, Beth. *Childless: The Hurt and the Hope*. Lion, 1989.

Stott, J. *Abortion*. Marshalls, 1985.

Williams, N. *False Images: Telling the Truth about Pornography*. Kingsway, 1991.

Wilson, Earl. *A Silence to be Broken*. Inter-Varsity Press, 1987.

2   Useful Addresses

Christian organisations

ACET (AIDS Care, Education and Training)
PO Box 1323, London W5 5TF.

British Council of Churches Community and Race Relations
Unit
2 Eaton Gate, London SW1W 9BL

CARE (Christian Action, Research and Education)
53 Romney Street London SW1P 3RF Tel: 071 233 0455

Causeway (Christian Concern for the Mentally Handicapped)
PO Box 351, Reading, Berkshire RG1 7AL Tel: 0734 508781

Christian Council on Ageing
Caponscleugh House, Allerwash, Fourstones, Hexham,
Northumberland NE47 5AB Tel: 0434 674271

Christian CND
22 Underwood Street, London N1 7JG Tel: 071 250 4010

Christian Medical Fellowship
157 Waterloo Road, London SE1 8XN. Tel: 071 928 4694.

Church Action With the Unemployed
45b Blythe Street, Bethnal Green, London E2 6LN Tel: 071
729 9990

Church Action on Disability
Charisma Cottage, Drewsteignton, Devon EX6 6QR

Church Action on Poverty
Central Buildings, Oldham Street, Manchester M1 1JT Tel:
061 236 9321

Disabled Christian Fellowship
211 Wick Road, Brislington, Bristol, Avon BS4 4HP Tel:
0272 720720

Evangelical Christians for Racial Justice
12 Bell barn Shopping Centre, Cregoe Street, Birmingham
B15 2DZ Tel: 021 622 5799

Evangelical Alliance
Whitefield House, 186 Kennington Park Road, London SE11
4BT Tel: 071 582 0228

Family Life and Marriage Education
28 Cromwell Road, Chesterfield, Derbyshire S40 4TH Tel:
0246 232937

Field Lane Foundation (centres for elderly, homeless,
disabled)
16 Vine Hill, Clerkenwell Road, London EC1R 5EA Tel:
071 837 0412

Grandma's (service for HIV infected and affected families)
PO Box 1392 London SW6 4EJ Tel: 071 731 0911

Industrial Christian Fellowship
St Katharine Kree Church, 86 Leadenhall Street, London
EC3A 3DH

Jubilee Campaigns (Campaigning on behalf of prisoners of
conscience)
PO Box 80, Cobham, Surrey KT11 2BQ Tel: 0932 67037

Jubilee Centre (Keep Sunday Special Campaign/Credit
Action)
3 Hooper Street, Cambridge CB1 2NZ Tel: 0223 311596

Living Waters UK (local church-based discipleship
programme with special emphasis on gender identity and
sexual issues)
PO Box 1530, London SW1W 0GW.

Movement for Christian Democracy
c/o David Alton MP, House of Commons, London
SW1A 0AP

Order of Christian Unity
58 Hanover Gardens, London SE11 Tel: 071 735 6210

Salvation Army Social Services
105 Judd Street, London WC1H 9TS Tel: 071 383 4230

Shaftesbury Society
18 Kingston Road, London SW19 1JZ Tel: 081 542 5550

Society for Protection of Unborn Children
Faith House, 17 Tufton Street, London SW1 Tel: 071 222
5845.

Stepping Stones Trust (for men who become Christians in
prison)
15 Westmead, London SW15 5BH Tel: 081 788 1450

Tear Fund
100 Church Road, Teddington, Middx TW11 8QE Tel: 081
977 9144.

West Indian Evangelical Alliance
71 Hayter Road, Brixton, London SW2 5AD

World Vision
Dept C092, Dychurch House, 8 Abingdon Street,
Northampton, NN1 2AJ. Tel: 0604 22964.

Education

Advisory Centre for Education
18 Victoria Park Square, London E2 9PB

Association of Christian Teachers
2 Romeland Hill, St Albans, Herts AL3 4ET

Association of Christian Teachers in Scotland
21 Rutland Square, Edinburgh EH1 2BB Tel: 031 229 8931

Christian Education Movement
Royal Buildings, Victoria Street, Derby DE1 1GW Tel: 0332
296655

Christians in Education (a division of CARE Trust)
CARE, 53 Romney Street, London SW1P 3RF Tel: 071 233
0455

The Christian Institute
PO Box 1, Newcastle-upon-Tyne NE7 7EF. Tel: 091 281 4544.

Christians in Science Education
John Bausor, CISE Secretary, 5 Longcroft Road, Edgware,
Middx HA8 6RR

Christian Schools Trust
Elmfield, Ambrose Lane, Harpenden, Herts AL5 4DA. Tel:
0582 765406.

Family and Youth Concern
Wicken Manor, Wicken, Nr Milton Keynes Tel: 0908 57234

National Confederation of Parent Teacher Associations
43 Stonebridge Road, Northfleet, Gravesend, Kent DA11
9DS

Scripture Union
130 City Road, London EC1V 2NJ

Stapleford House
Wesley Place, Stapleford, Nottingham NG9 8DP Tel: 0602
396270

General

Age Concern
60 Pitcairn Road, Mitcham, Surrey CR4 3LL Tel: 081 640
5431

Charities Aid Foundation
48 Pembury Road, Tonbridge, Kent TN9 2JD Tel: 0732 771
333

Child Poverty Action Group
4th Floor, 1–5 Bath Street, London EC1V 9PY Tel: 071 253
3406

Children's Society
Edward Rudolph House, Margery Street, London WC1X
0JL

Friends of the Earth
26–28 Underwood Street, London N1 7JQ Tel: 071 490 1555

Greenpeace
30–31 Islington Green, London N1 8XE Tel: 071 354 5100

Help the Aged
St James Walk, London EC1R 0BE Tel: 071 253 0253

LIFE
118–120 Warwick Street, Leamington Spa, Warwickshire.
Tel: 0926 21587

MENCAP
123 Golden Lane, London EC1Y 0RT Tel: 071 253 9433

Mental Health Foundation
8 Hallam Street, London W1N 6DH

Money Advice Association
20 Grosvenor Gardens, London SW1W 0DH Tel: 071 730
3469

NACRO (National Association for the Care and Resettle-
ment of Offenders)
169 Clapham Road, London SW9 0PU Tel: 071 278 9815

National Council for Voluntary Organisations
26 Bedford Square, London WC1B 3HW Tel: 071 636 4066

National Association of Citizen's Advice Bureaux
Myddleton House, 115–123 Pentonville Road, London N1
9LZ Tel: 071 833 2181

National Federation of Housing Associations
175 Grays Inn Road, London WC1H 8LR Tel: 071 833 2071

NSPCC
67 Saffron Hill, London EC1N 8RS Tel: 071 242 1626

PHAB
Tavistock House North, Tavistock Square, London WC1H
9HX Tel: 071 388 1963

Royal College of Obstetricians and Gynaecologists
27 Sussex Place, London NW1 Tel: 071 262 5425

Shelter
88 Old Street, London EC1V 9HU Tel: 071 253 0202

Simon Community
St Joseph's House, 129 Malden Road, London NW5 4HS
Tel: 071 485 6639

World Development Movement
Bedford Chambers, Covent Garden, London WC2E 8HA
Tel 071 836 3672

Government, public offices and organisations of public interest

Association of County Councils
Eaton House, 66A Eaton Square, London SW1W 9BH Tel:
071 235 1200

Association of Metropolitan Authorities
35 Great Smith Street, London SW1P 3BJ Tel: 071 222 8100

Association for Neighbourhood Councils
50 Whetstone Close, Farquhar Road, Edgbaston, Birmingham
B15 2QN Tel: 021 454 8128

British Medical Association
BMA House, Tavistock Square, London WC1 Tel: 071 387 4499

Department of the Environment
Marsham Towers, Marsham Street, London SW1 Tel: 071 212 3434

Department of Trade and Industry
Victoria Street, London SW1 Tel: 071 215 7877

Department of Social Security
Alexander Fleming House, Elephant and Castle, London SE1 Tel: 071 407 5522

Department for National Heritage (responsible for broadcasting, sport, arts, museums, national lotteries)
Horseguards Road, London SW1P 3AL Tel: 071 270 3000

Department of Transport
2 Marsham Street, London SW1P 3EB Tel: 071 276 3000

Department of Employment
Caxton House, Tothill Street, London SW1H 9NF
Tel: 071 273 3000

European Parliament Information Office
United Kingdom Office, 2 Queen Anne's Gate, London SW1H 9AA Tel: 071 222 0411

European Commission Information Offices
8 Storey's Gate, London SW1P 3AT;
Windsor House, 9/15 Bedford Street, Belfast BT2 7EG;
4 Cathedral Road, Cardiff CF1 9SG;
7 Alva Street, Edinburgh EH2 4PH.

Foreign Office
King Charles Street, London SW1 Tel: 071 233 3000

Home Office
Queen Anne's Gate, London SW1 Tel: 071 213 3000

Prime Minister's Office
10 Downing Street, London SW1A 2AA Tel: 071 930 4433

Northern Ireland Office
Whitehall, London SW1A 2AZ Tel: 071 210 3000
Stormont Castle, Belfast BT4 3ST Tel: 0232 763255

Scottish Office
Dover House, Whitehall, London SW1A 2AU Tel: 071 270 3000
St Andrew's House, Edinburgh EH1 3DE Tel: 031 556 8400

Welsh Office
Gwydyr House, Whitehall, London SW1A 2ER Tel: 071 270 3000
There are also offices in Cardiff and Aberystwyth.

Association of District Councils
26 Chapter Street, London SW1P 4ND Tel: 071 233 6868

Association of London Authorities
36 Old Queen Street, London SW1 9JF Tel: 071 222 7799

Association of Local Authorities in Northern Ireland
123 York Street, Belfast BT15 1AB Tel: 0232 249286

Health Education Council
78 New Oxford Street, London WC1A 1AH Tel: 071 631 0930

Her Majesty's Stationery Office
St Crispin's, Duke Street, Norwich NR3 1PD Tel: 0603 22211

Office of Population, Censuses and Surveys
St Catherine's House, 10 Kingsway, London WC2B 6JP
Tel: 071 242 0262

Attorney-General
The Attorney-General's Chambers, Royal Courts of Justice,
The Strand, London WC2A 2LL Tel: 071 936 6000

Crown Office (Scotland)
5–7 Regents Road, Edinburgh EH7 5BL Tel: 031 557 3800

Director of Public Prosecutions
4–12 Queen Anne's Gate, London SW1H 9AZ Tel: 071 213
3000

House of Commons
Westminster, London SW1A 0AA Tel: 071 219 4272
(Information Office); 071 219 3000 (Central Switchboard)

House of Lords
Westminster, London SW1A 0YW Tel: 071 219 3107
(Information Office)

Law Commission
Conquest House, 37–38 John Street, Theobalds Road,
London WC1N 2BQ Tel: 071 242 0861

Lord Advocates Department (Scotland)
Fielden House, 10 Great College Street, Westminster,
London SW1P 3LS Tel: 071 212 7676

Lord Chancellor
The House of Lords, London SW1A 0YW Tel: 071 219 3000

Lord Chief Justice
Royal Courts of Justice, The Strand, London WC2A 2LL
Tel: 071 936 6000

Scottish Law Commission
140 Causewayside, Edinburgh EH9 1PR Tel: 031 668 2131

Scotland Yard
New Scotland Yard, Broadway, London SW1H 0BG Tel:
071 230 1212

Solicitor-General
The House of Commons, London SW1A 0AA Tel: 071 219
3000

Direct Mail Services Standards Board
26 Eccleston Street, London SW1W 9PY Tel: 071 824 8651

Political parties

Alliance Party of Northern Ireland
88 University Street, Belfast Tel: 0232 224274

Conservative Party
Central Office, 32 Smith Square, London SW1P 3HH Tel:
071 222 9000

Ulster Democratic Unionist Party
296 Albertbridge Road, Belfast BT5 4PY Tel: 0232 58597

Green Party
10 Station Parade, Balham High Road, London SW12 9HZ
Tel: 081 673 0045

Labour Party
150 Walworth Road, London SE17 1JT Tel: 071 703 0833

Liberal Democrats
4 Cowley Street, London SW1P 3NB Tel: 071 222 7999

Plaid Cymru
51 Cathedral Road, Cardiff CF1 9HD Tel: 0222 31944

Social Democratic Labour Party
24 Mount Chanes, Belfast BT7 1NZ Tel: 0232 323428

Scottish Conservative and Unionist Party
Suite 1/1, 14 Links Place, Leith, Edinburgh EH6 7EZ
Tel: 031 555 2869

Scottish Liberal Democrats
4 Clifton Terrace, Edinburgh EH12 5DR Tel: 031 337 2314

Scottish National Party
6 North Charlotte Street, Edinburgh EH2 4JH Tel: 031 226
3661

Ulster Unionist Party
3 Glangall Street, Belfast BT12 5AE Tel: 0232 224601

Welsh Liberal Democrats
57 St Mary's Street, Cardiff CF1 1FE Tel: 0222 382210

Media

Advertising Standards Authority
Brook House, Torrington Place, London WC1 Tel: 071 580 5555

BBC TV Wales
Broadcasting House, Llandaff, Cardiff CF5 2YQ Tel: 0222
564888

BBC TV Northern Ireland
Broadcasting House, Ormeau Avenue, Belfast BT2 8HQ
Tel: 0232 244400

BBC TV Scotland
Broadcasting House, Queen Margaret Drive, Glasgow G12
8BG Tel: 041 339 8844

BBC Television Centre
Wood Lane, Shepherds Bush, London W12 Tel: 081 743 8000

BBC Radio
Broadcasting House, Portland Place, London W1A 1AA Tel:
071 580 4468

British Board of Film Classification
3 Soho Square, London W1 Tel: 071 439 7961

Broadcasting Standards Council
5–8 The Sanctuary, London SW1P 3JS Tel: 071 233 0455

Channel Four Television Company
60 Charlotte St, London W1P 2AX Tel: 071 631 4444

Independent Television Commission
70 Brompton Road, London SW3 1EY
(The ITC are able to tell you the name and address of the
commercial television company operating in your area.)

National Viewers and Listeners Association
Blahernae, Ardleigh, Colchester CO7 7RH Tel: 0206 230123

Press Complaints Commission
1 Salisbury Square, London EC4Y 8AE Tel: 071 353 1248

Radio Authority
3rd Floor, 70 Brompton Road, London SW3 1EY Tel: 071
581 2888

Index

Into The Arena

by Paul Miller

They say you should never discuss politics or religion if you don't want to argue. *Into the Arena* shows why.

Down through the ages people have tried to formulate models of society that are just and compassionate. Differences of opinion have been sharp, as each model has assumed its own view of morality. And when God comes into the picture, the debate hots up still further. Just how should God's law relate to secular society?

Paul Miller skilfully reviews the classical models of a godly society and goes on to examine present-day attempts to bring a Christian voice to the public arena. His arguments are compelling, while his conclusions—if implemented—could pave the way for a more truly Christian dimension to the shared life of our nation.

'For more than a decade many evangelical Christian leaders have been urging believers to abandon their traditional isolation from "secular society". *Into the Arena* is a must for those who hope to have a Christian influence in the political life of their nation.'
—LYNN GREEN
Youth With A Mission
Director for Europe, Middle East & Africa

'Can a book about political involvement be readable, lively, well-researched, biblical and challenging? You'd be forgiven if your answer was no; but Paul Miller has written such a book.'
LYNDON BOWRING
Chairman, CARE Trust

Kingsway Publications